PRAISE FOR *YOUR C*
DIFFERENTLY, NOW WHAT!

"At last! A definitive guide for parents to understand and use cognitive skills training to level the playing field for their children who learn differently. In one easy-to-read book, expert authors Hill and Stark have wiped the slate clean and given parents a leg up they have so desperately been searching for."

—**Charles Sosnik,** education analyst and syndicated columnist

"I have seen happy children reach their full potential no matter what their learning difficulties. I offer my congratulations to Stark and Hill for tackling such a difficult issue in this book and for what they have done for children everywhere."

—**Dr. Patricia Wolfe,** author, *Brain Matters*

"Roger Stark and Betsy Hill's new book *Your Child Learns Differently, Now What?* gets at the real juggernaut in American education around success for all in our K-12 education system. The authors clearly identify and provide interventions for the critical mental processes called cognitive skills, the basis of how our brain learns, a topic too little discussed in teacher preparation programs. If your child is struggling in school, especially at the elementary grades, you want to devour the knowledge and skills Stark and Hill have presented."

—**Dr. Kenneth Eastwood,** former superintendent, Middletown City School District, New York

"This book leaves one so hopeful for helping children at all stages of the learning process. It addresses parents' pain, pressures, strengths and appeals to their commitment to 'take the wheel' and use the mindset and practical skills described and validated with such impactful statistics and facts. This book is filled with real stories, real pain, real solutions."

—**Kathy Leck,** executive coach, adjunct professor, Lake Forest Graduate School of Management

"Once I started reading *Your Child Learns Differently, Now What?* I did not put the book down aside from driving home from work and dinner with my family. Everyone can learn better and be a better student. It happens for us with our students, in an average small town, with kids of all backgrounds. They stop being tardy, they are more organized, and the discipline and poor choices dissolve."

—**Gregg Goewert, Ed.S.,** principal, Urey Middle School, Walkerton, Indiana

"Roger and Betsy bring hope to those in the desert of learning distress through this thought-provoking read! Everyone can truly be the CEO of You. The keys to unlock this hope are within."

—**Mark Bowell,** parent, school board member, president, The Institute for Learning Dynamics

"A light for caregivers that are willing to help their loved ones shine in school and life. Read and succeed!"

—**John Axtell,** Homeschooler, Special Education Mentor and Advocate, School Board Member

"As a middle school principal, I often look for ways for my
teachers to change and modify their practices, or for a new
curricular tool to help make data more actionable, but
never had I considered the possibility of a tool designed to
help the students instead. BrainWare came to my school
back in 2019 and I was hopefully optimistic. I had tried
other programs and it always seemed they would
overpromise and underdeliver with regard to meaningful
impact on student success. Within the first five months of
implementation, it was easy to see something was different
about BrainWare. Throughout the past four years of using
and implementing BrainWare in my school, I have learned
so much about the 'why' of student struggles, as well as
ways to overcome the educational hurdles that may pop
up. If students are academically behind when they get to
middle school, there are likely barriers that exist in their
cognitive processes. And despite all the best intentions,
until you are able to help them overcome and learn new
strategies, you will continue to watch those same issues
keep them from the success they desire and deserve.
Your Child Learns Differently walks through the what, why
and how of student struggles and gives you the tools to
overcome before the gap becomes too large to close."

—**Tom Hughes,** principal, Maple Crest STEM Middle
School, Kokomo, Indiana

"I am so glad that Betsy and Roger have shared their
knowledge and expertise in this area. The parent
testimonials are very moving and help what they are
teaching have more impact."

—**Dr. Laurie S. Lipman,** psychiatrist affiliated with
Northwestern Medicine-Northwestern Memorial
Hospital, Chicago, Illinois

"What an incredible book! Parents, grandparents, and guardians will find it valuable. Not only does it go into detail about what cognitive skills are, it explains that they are the foundation for all learning and why it's so important that we help our children develop these skills. It's an easy read and the personal stories clearly make it easy for parents to understand why their child might be struggling and how to help them."

—**Dr. Lou Whitaker,** retired associate superintendent, principal and teacher

"I really enjoyed reading this book. It is well written, very informative, impactful and inspiring. It is a valuable resource that will enhance parents' ability to build their children's learning ability so that learning becomes engaging, fun, and intellectually liberating."

—**Donald Newman,** CEO, CRG Capital

Your Child Learns Differently, Now What?

Your Child Learns Differently, Now What?

The Truth for Parents

ROGER STARK AND BETSY HILL

SEABISCUIT PRESS

CHICAGO

SEABISCUIT PRESS

ISBN: 979-8-9871882-0-0 (PAPERBACK)
ISBN: 979-8-9871882-1-7 (HARDCOVER)
ISBN: 979-8-9871882-2-4 (EBOOK)

Manufactured in the United States of America

FIRST EDITION

I dedicate this book to my mother, who inspired me to use my resources to help others. I also dedicate it to every family who is touched by it in any way. May your children find their paths to success in our world. I am honored to have a place on their paths as you help them do better in school and grow up to be people you and they can be proud of. May you find encouragement and support on every page.

—Roger Stark

For Charlotte and Emma, my granddaughters, who express the joy of learning in everything they do.

—Betsy Hill

CONTENTS

CHAPTER TWO
Step #1 Take the Wheel   25

CHAPTER THREE
Step #2 Set High Standards   45

CHAPTER FOUR
Step #3 Build the Cognitive Foundation for Learning

FOREWORD

Science tells us that anything with strong emotion is remembered much longer and in much more detail than mundane everyday events. Perhaps that's why I remember my third year of teaching when I was given a first-grade class. After having focused on socialization in my previous kindergarten classes, I was excited to have the opportunity to focus on teaching children to read. I knew that being able to read formed the basis of future success in school. I also remember how proud I was in first grade when I finished reading my first Dick and Jane book. This was going to be an exciting year!

Unfortunately, it was not the joyful experience I anticipated. Yes, I did teach some children to read and to calculate and to engage successfully in simple science experiments. However, there were some students I was not able to reach no matter what I tried. I went back over the books I had read in my teacher preparation classes but found no answers. I talked to more experienced teachers and discovered that they were as puzzled as I was at why some students learned so easily and why others struggled and failed. It didn't seem to be linked to intellectual capacity or to any other particular factor like ADHD or autism.

It wasn't until after many more years of teaching children and a new job teaching teachers that I began to find some answers to the problems all teachers face. At a conference, I heard a researcher talk about the brain's memory systems. It was a "Eureka moment." Perhaps the answer to why some children learned easily and others did not could be found in an understanding of the human brain. Indeed, this hunch proved to be true. There are many brain functions involved in learning. Among them are visual perception, auditory processing, sensory integration, attention, memory and executive functions. These functions are components of a broad category labeled cognitive skills. A problem in any one of these functions of the brain can cause significant learning deficits. However, the average teacher or parent does not have the skills to assess children to identify their strengths and weaknesses and even if they did, they would not have the skills to ameliorate the deficits or take advantage of the strengths.

This was the puzzle that intrigued Roger Stark. Think how many children he could help if he could find the answer to the puzzle. It took years of research, but Roger has accomplished the enormous task of incorporating the diagnostic work of experts (and the strategies they used in their private practices to improve cognitive functioning) into an engaging video game, BrainWare SAFARI.

With his collaborator, Betsy Hill, Roger has tested the program throughout the United States with very satisfying results. As you read this book, you'll be fascinated by the testimonials of parents and teachers who have used BrainWare with their children and their classes. You'll have the opportunity to read the rigorous research that Stark and Hill have done, and the positive findings of their studies.

I very seldom recommend a program to teachers or parents. Few programs are based on neuroscience and almost none have research backing. But I am delighted to recommend

BrainWare. I have seen happy children reach their full potential no matter what their learning difficulties. I offer my congratulations to both Stark and Hill for tackling such a difficult issue and for what they have done for children everywhere.

Pat Wolfe, Ed.D.
President: Brain Matters, Inc.
Author: *Brain Matters; Translating Research to Classroom Practice*

ACKNOWLEDGMENTS

We offer special thanks to all of the people in our lives who contributed in so many ways to the writing of this book and to the experiences that led up to it. They include Dr. Sarah Avtzon, Julie Blake, Florence Boots, Mark Bowell, Kris Bowen, Karen Buccola, Florence Cox, William Erickson, Andrew Hill, Jeremy Hill, Zachary Hill, Dave Jordan, Peter Klein, Charles Lynn, Maulsey Lillian Lynn, David MacKenzie, Sheila Myrcik, Dr. Alan Nishino, Dr. Russ Osnes, Susan Perkins, Dr. Sara Sawtelle, Annette Simmons, Charles Sosnik, Jeffery Thomas, Dr. Gary Vogel, Dr. Lou Whitaker, and Dr. Pat Wolfe.

KEY TO SYMBOLS

Case Study

Parent or Kid's Quote

Expert's Quote

Parent Key

One of the ways we'll unpack the learning process is by revealing Parent Keys to unlocking the truth of learning. You will find these throughout the book.

INTRODUCTION

"We've seen huge success with our son. Number one, with his self-confidence, which I think has been huge for him to even be able to learn. Instead of withdrawing and shutting down because 'Oh, I just don't know it. I don't understand,' he doesn't just shut down right away so much anymore. He's pushing himself because he has confidence, and that confidence is coming from BrainWare and the coach's one-on-one sessions. That's been the best thing.

"He's been participating more, and he started comprehending more and therefore communicating more. Overall, just a much happier kid.

"It seemed like almost after the first or second session, we could kind of see a little bit of improvement but then big time after a few months. And his teachers at school are starting to notice that he's interacting more, engaging more with assignments and the teachers and the class in general. It's not just us noticing; it's other people too.

"Seeing all this success with the program and seeing Tyler reacting to it, I mean it just makes us so happy. It's been a long road. As parents, you worry are you doing the right thing and doing the best, and you just keep trying so hard. To see that we've found something that really works for him and that he loves it ... I've heard reviews from other programs, but he never got it with them. To finally find one has been, for me, super exciting. I feel so successful, and I'm just so happy because he's happy and improving. We all learn differently. We're all different people, and what's amazing is that he's happy.

"What I would say to parents that have a child or children that struggle with, you know, all sorts of things, there's all kinds of things that a teacher will comment on and tell you to work on, from ADHD to autism, to developmental delays, to speech therapy ...

"What I would say is don't ever give up, don't stop trying, keep going. There's something out there for everybody. We're all different, so what may work for our son may not work for somebody else. However, I think because I had tried so many programs for pretty much eight years, doing as much research as I've done and trying pretty much everything, I would recommend don't give up and try this, even if everything else has failed. We had tried everything – luckily, we had the financial means to do that – and this has just been the best.

"I wish I would've known about this before when he was younger. Probably he would not have struggled as much and maybe even be at grade level. So, I just encourage you – don't give up, keep going, and please try this program because it has done an amazing job not just for his academics but for his psychosocial and mental well-being, just for everything."

—Michelle and Brian Stilphen,
parents of Tyler (age nine)

This story may sound like a miracle, and in fact, it is. Yet, it happens every day.

Children around the world struggle in school. Their parents hire tutors, help with homework or fight nightly homework battles. They do everything they can to help their child complete assignments, prepare for tests and bring up their grades. Parents often ask their child's teacher for help. Too often, it doesn't work; the teacher doesn't seem to have the answers either.

Chances are you are in a similar situation, and you are reading this book hoping for answers. Let us assure you that you are in the right place. We have worked with thousands of families whose children struggle in school and out of school. We know that you want the best for your child. We understand how hard you have tried. We feel what you feel when you reach the end of your rope, as have many parents we work with.

You may be reading this at the end of a long, trying day after work and dealing with the kids. You've poured your heart, soul, time, and money into helping your child, but nothing has made much of a difference. Your child may be discouraged, anxious or easily frustrated by what seem like straightforward learning tasks. You may feel your heart break every time they cover their face and tell you, "I'm stupid. I can't do this."

In short, it's time for something different. It's time to understand why some children sail through school assignments and others labor through them. It's time to dispel commonly held myths about learning – like everyone learns the same, it just takes some longer. In reality, every child learns differently. Without this understanding, you will look long and hard for a solution.

This book will help you understand the pieces of the learning puzzle. The learning puzzle may seem like a great mystery when you attend those parent-teacher conferences or listen to the principal of your child's school discuss their educational priorities. But once you understand how brains learn and uncover how your child's brain learns best, several important things happen.

First, you get more insight into your child, and when you have that insight, you can help in real ways. Often, parents also develop more patience when they have this insight. Let's face it. When your child doesn't do what you ask them to do, it can be hard to have a lot of patience. When you understand why (for example, because their brains just can't hold on to your instructions long enough for them to carry them out), and when you know what to do about it, patience comes naturally.

Second, you start to see how the school system fails your child by focusing on teaching rather than learning. As you'll learn through the pages of this book, the education system puts its efforts and resources into curriculum, instruction, technology and the like. It usually doesn't address the number one factor that affects student outcomes. We'll tell you what that is in just a minute.

Third, you see your child overcome their struggles to succeed not just in school but in the rest of their life, too. And in ways that will carry over into adulthood.

Finally, your stress and anxiety dissolve as you realize that the struggles you have been wrangling with can be gone forever.

By the way, your child is not the only one our schools are failing. Only about 35 percent of fourth graders are reading proficiently at grade level in the U.S., and not much has changed in decades of "educational progress." But for now, let's focus on you and your child.

This book is for parents of:

- Struggling learners. This book is for parents of kids who struggle with learning, whether at school or at home. There is usually a reason when children struggle with learning, even if no one is talking about it.

- Students who learn differently. The fact of the matter is that every one of us learns uniquely. Many, if not most, students have learning skills that fall outside what the education system counts on students bringing to the classroom. So many times, that's what it's actually about – learning differently. When you are with your child every single day, you know the great capacity they have to be special. But sometimes, sitting in that classroom every day, they just don't quite get what's coming at them the way it's being presented. It doesn't mean they're stupid or they're incapable. In fact, you know they're bright and capable, even if it's not translating to school and even if they can't recognize it themselves, so they struggle.

- Hard-working learners. They may spend hours on their homework. They don't complain. They get good grades. But their families know they're just working too hard for the results they get. They agonize over every bit of learning. Maybe they have been written off as a perfectionist, but you know as their parent that something is blocking their learning potential. And you know if that barrier were gone, they could do exceptionally well, with much less effort.

The truth is that every child has unique learning strengths and weaknesses. On average, schools succeed with about a third of them. The other two-thirds range from students with learning disabilities to gifted students (and some are both!). Until you understand how your child learns and have a plan to help them tap into their unique learning strengths, everything you (and their teachers) do will be hit or miss. And every time it's a miss, your child loses confidence and drive.

So, if you're a parent who truly wants to help your child

overcome the barriers that stand in the way of them reaching their full potential, this is for you. And we're excited to share how to do so in this book.

You will learn how to determine the real reasons your child struggles with learning and how to identify their unique learning strengths. What's critical is to uncover those strengths and weaknesses, build and strengthen the weak areas, and make the strengths even stronger.

To do this, we'll unpack the learning process – without all the mumbo jumbo – so you can clearly understand the role of learning capacity.

While we'll avoid technical language as much as we can, there is one term that we need to introduce right from the get-go, and that is the term "cognitive skills."

- Cognitive skills are the processes our brains use to take in information from the outside world and understand, organize, store, retrieve and apply that information.

- Cognitive skills are HOW we learn.

- Cognitive skills are also the number one factor that impacts student outcomes.

One of the ways we'll unpack the learning process is by revealing parent keys to unlocking the truth of learning. You will find these throughout the book, and here is the first. (By the way, you can find all of the Parent Keys in the book collected in Appendix 2.)

PARENT KEY 1

Cognitive skills account for 50 percent of the variance in students' academic performance. That means that half of the difference between one child's academic performance and the child sitting next to them can be predicted by their cognitive skills. Not teachers, not class size, not curriculum or technology. So, if two students go to the same school for 13 years and one gets As, and the other gets Ds, half of that difference is explained by their learning capacity, more than any other factor.

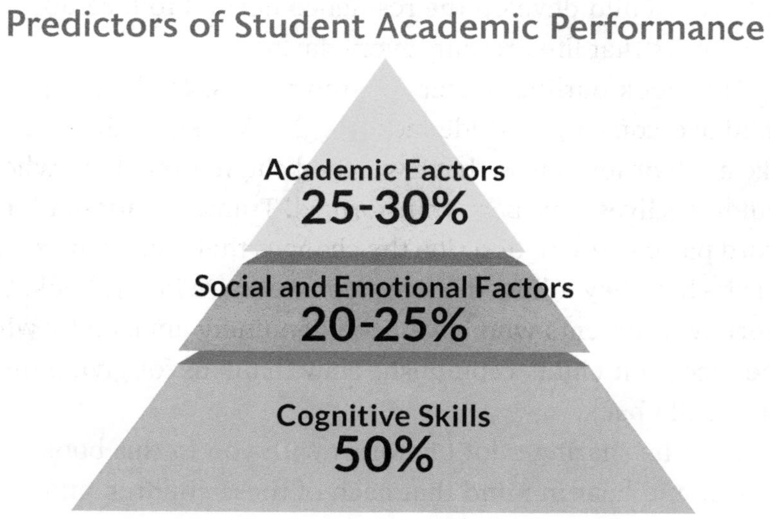

Predictors of Student Academic Performance

Academic Factors
25-30%

Social and Emotional Factors
20-25%

Cognitive Skills
50%

Figure 1: Cognitive skills are the foundation of learning and account for 50 percent of the variability of learning outcomes.

In this book, you will learn how you can take charge and build the best learning capacity for your child. We will explain why learning issues and behavioral issues are often two sides of the same coin. Students who struggle with learning often also exhibit behavior issues. They may act out. They may shut down. Schools and parents tend to look at academic and behavior issues as if they were completely separate. But they are almost always closely related. Your child has one brain, and it's very systemic in nature. So, all of these systems work together.

You will learn how our clients build up their children's confidence. Confidence is so important. Your struggling learner may have lost confidence, had their self-esteem stolen from them. You will discover how to uplift their spirits and get them fully engaged in their schoolwork and family life. You will discover the true nature of grit and perseverance. And see how to help your child develop the resilience needed to face difficult challenges that life presents every day.

This book outlines a step-by-step process for helping your child overcome their academic struggles. We know that sounds like a tall order, but we have watched client after client whose children's lives have been transformed. Transformation. It's the word parents use to describe the changes their children experience when they follow the five steps we share in this book. We work with parents who have been genuinely amazed by what they see their child accomplish. They thank us for giving them their child back.

We'll be sharing a lot of stories with you in this book, and you should bear in mind that each of these children and their families is unique. No two experiences are the same, and each child's individual development and circumstances will vary. These days, everybody's looking for the magic pill and the quick fix, but there's no silver bullet here. There's no magic pill for this effort. It's going to take work, but will it be rewarding work! In fact, it will probably be the most rewarding work you'll ever do in your entire life. It will be the greatest gift you will ever give your child – a gift that gives for a lifetime.

"I think that all kids have strengths and weaknesses, and they feel much better about their weaknesses when they know their strengths. BrainWare SAFARI did that for Matt. I had a hard time believing the results because he showed such a huge amount of improvement. I took him to a psychologist because I wanted to validate the results. They were all validated. I was just the happiest mom in town."

—Barb M., mother of Matt (age nine)

Probably the thing we've heard most from parents in the past few years is how hard it was for kids to do school online. But MOST IMPORTANTLY, we've heard what parents learned from watching their kids struggle. In many cases, it was unexpected. With children expected to learn remotely from home, parents could see their children falling behind and not getting support.

But the problem isn't just the impact of the COVID-19 pandemic. Likely you can identify with some of these situations:

- All those freshly sharpened pencils and new school clothes and new friends that ring in a new school year are not the real stuff of school. For many families, the new school year doesn't really offer a fresh start. The same concerns and disappointments start to emerge even before that first report card.

- Or perhaps you're like many parents who dread parent-teacher conferences because they are full of problems and no solutions are offered. Just Lincoln or Christina needs to work a little harder. Most of the time, the true solution is not about working harder.

- Many of the families we've worked with have sought help from a parade of tutors or months or years of tutoring services without seeing any real change.

- And you've probably been through nightly homework battles or meltdowns. You despair over how to get your child through an assignment and into bed without the roof caving in.

- The family arguments over your child's learning struggles make other relationships difficult. Your partner, parents, in-laws or other children all seem to have something to say on the topic. The stress of learning struggles often affects everyone in the family.

- Often, parents have been through what we sometimes call the gauntlet. If problems have been uncovered early, perhaps you've been to a series of experts or other therapists. If we had a nickel for every parent who's said to us, "They just tell me what's wrong, they don't tell me what to do about it," we would be ridiculously rich.

So, here's the real problem.

The real problem is that you haven't yet learned the five steps we will share in this book.

Once you take them, you can sleep well at night, knowing that you can send your child off to school the next morning, and in fact, every morning, confident that they have the skills to succeed and to bounce back from challenges. You can see that smile on your child's face when they figure out the answer to a homework problem, all by themselves. You can watch your child start to blossom and come into their own. You can look forward to parent-teacher conferences and hearing how much your child has grown. You can hear them start to participate in dinner table conversations with their own insights.

"I'll tell you it was truly an act of the Holy Spirit. I was feeling really frustrated about 15 months ago in my role. I love working with students with learning disabilities; however, I always felt like I was just patching and trying to get through the next assignment or the next assessment and just teach those concepts. Often, I turned to my colleagues or my husband at home, and I would say, 'You know, I can't fix their brains, so all I can do is continue to patch and patch and patch and move along. Out of nowhere, I received an email announcement about a webinar about this program called BrainWare SAFARI. This professor out of New York had used the program with an experimental group of LD [learning disabled] students. And she used a control group as well. The gains that her students had made after using the program were really impressive.

"I will say that, truly, finding this program changed my professional life. I'm not being dramatic or exaggerating when I say that. I had come to a point where I had given up hope about my profession. I felt I was spinning my wheels and really wasn't making much of a difference long-term. This has given me a reason to feel that what I do is truly important and meaningful, with long-term, long-lasting effects.

"It started with my experience with my son. The bottom line is that this has been his most successful year in school ever. His communication skills have increased enormously to the point that he can identify when he doesn't understand something, and he can articulate it. He remembers what to bring home from school, which was a real struggle for him previously. And something that is so pleasant for me as a parent, at the dinner table he's able to participate in conversations with us and really follow the flow of conversation, interject, ask questions ... that I really, really credit BrainWare SAFARI with."

—Stacy Mulrenin, resource teacher and mother

ABOUT THE AUTHORS

THE BACKSTORY

Over fifty years ago, a hearing specialist and a vision development specialist started talking. They soon learned that they were both frustrated by what they couldn't do for their clients. Both offered in-depth cognitive tests. Both told parents exactly why their children struggled in school. The tests also explained other behavioral problems.

The parents were pleased with the answers but always asked, "Now what can we do about it?" The doctors didn't have a lot to suggest. They started spending time with each other to share their ideas and approaches. They were convinced that they needed to work together, even though there was no proof yet of the importance of a multidisciplinary approach.

Along the way, other clinicians joined them. Speech pathologists, neurologists, psychologists, and other learning specialists joined in. Over about forty years of trial and error refining their ideas, they developed a set of one-on-one, mostly paper-and-pencil exercises. They used these exercises in their offices to help children with learning issues. There was no formal research at the time, yet they saw results. They watched the exercises help tens of thousands of children.

Enter Roger Stark.

Roger Stark is CEO of BrainWare Learning Company. For almost two decades, he has championed the effort to bring comprehensive cognitive skills assessment and training within reach of everyone. It started with a very basic question: What do we know about the brain? From that initial question, he pioneered the effort to build an effective and affordable cognitive skills training tool based on over forty years of trial-and-error clinical collaboration. Stark led the team that developed BrainWare SAFARI, which has become the world's most researched, comprehensive, integrated cognitive training tool delivered online.

Stark brought a unique background to this effort. He had played an active role in the early stages of the video game industry. He launched Steven Spielberg's first games before there was DreamWorks. He worked with early titles for E.A. Sports, Tiger Interactive (now part of Hasbro) and Namco Cybertainment.

Roger imagined a way to take that paper-and-pencil cognitive training program and deliver it in a video-game format. If it could be done – and that was a big if, at the time – it could help far more people. That was the birth of BrainWare SAFARI and the transformative changes that have been experienced by thousands of individuals, from those that struggle with learning to the gifted.

Enter Betsy Hill.

Betsy Hill is the president and COO of BrainWare Learning Company. Her fascination with the brain started at an early age. She followed the literature on the brain and language from college. She has taught at the elementary, secondary, university undergraduate and graduate levels. She has studied the application of neuroscience to learning and teaching with Dr. Patricia Wolfe (author of *Brain Matters*) and other pioneers in the field. Today she works with parents, educators, clinicians and corporate trainers on using neuroscience research to address some of the most perplexing problems in education, including closing the gap for historically underperforming students. She addressed issues of college and career preparedness as a trustee and board chair at Chicago State University. She holds a master of arts in teaching and an MBA from Northwestern University. She teaches strategic thinking at Lake Forest Graduate School of Management.

When Betsy joined Roger in the cause of bringing the BrainWare message to families and schools, BrainWare SAFARI was undergoing the first study of its impact on learning capacity. It would be the first of many conducted under Hill's leadership. Since joining the cause, Hill has written hundreds of articles, white papers and research reports. She has trained thousands of parents, teachers, administrators, clinicians and learning specialists in brain-compatible instructional practice and the role of cognitive skills in learning. She specializes in helping parents and educators apply the science of learning to improve academic and life outcomes.

OUR INSPIRATION

We envision a world where everyone can succeed in school and in life because they have developed the cognitive capacity to do so.

Many jobs of the future have not even been imagined yet. Our education system can't train future workers for specific jobs because we simply don't know what those jobs will be.

To be successful in the jobs of the future, our children and their children after them will need to be good thinkers and problem-solvers. They will need to be flexible in their thinking and have strong powers of observation and analysis. They will need to be capable learners because they will have to learn their jobs to do them, and then relearn them in a rapidly changing world. Their ability to learn fast, efficiently and effectively may very well be the number one factor in career success and advancement.

We expect to play a vital role in this process by focusing on the cognitive skills that are the foundation for learning. (Definitions of the 43 cognitive skills developed in BrainWare SAFARI are provided in Appendix 1.)

OUR BELIEFS

1. Learning is what counts. Teaching is only important if learning is taking place.

2. Learning requires a solid foundation. Cognitive skills are the foundation for learning. Cognitive skills can be thought of as learning capacity.

3. Everyone has the ability to learn, but not everyone has developed the same capacity for learning. We all have cognitive strengths and weaknesses, and we have brains that have developed uniquely through our interaction with the world around us.

4. Cognitive skills or a person's capacity to learn can be developed much more than most people think. Intelligence is not fixed.

5. Students who learn differently deserve more than workarounds like extra time and easier work. They deserve to build their learning capacity. The potential to build learning capacity may be the most underutilized asset in our education system.

6. Education and economic security are closely tied together. Doing well in school helps students realize their earning potential. But growing up in poverty is associated with less well-developed cognitive skills.

The long-standing educational performance gaps for students who are economically disadvantaged can be closed, raising their lifetime earning potential.

7. Achievement gaps are strongly related with cognitive gaps. Access to learning experiences relies on well-developed cognitive skills, among other factors. Helping every individual develop their cognitive skills is a matter of equity.

8. Cognitive skills and mental health are closely related. Some diseases and conditions are accompanied by cognitive impairment and others, such as anxiety, can be the result of learning struggles.

9. Learning struggles affect families, not just the individual who struggles with learning. Lowering the stress and anxiety of a child by helping them become a capable and confident learner can decrease the stress level for the entire family.

10. Developing cognitive skills efficiently, and in a way that yields lasting, meaningful results, can be achieved with the right kind of cognitive training. The right kind of cognitive training takes a comprehensive, multi-disciplinary approach, integrating the best practices from clinical and educational psychology, auditory and vision developmental therapy, occupational therapy, speech and language pathology, neurology and other disciplines.

11. Learning should be fun and cognitive training should be engaging and motivating. The use of video-game technology can play an important role in effective cognitive training, but "brain games" are not cognitive training.

12. Research on program effectiveness is an ongoing responsibility. It is incumbent on us as the developer and provider of cognitive assessment, cognitive training and other cognitively based learning programs, to continue to demonstrate their effectiveness, with a meaningful impact for the clients we serve, and in keeping with the evolution of the science of learning.

A Message from Roger Stark

My passion is helping kids who struggle in school or feel like life hasn't been fair to them. I tell them, "Do not accept the victim mentality! Yes, your environment, experiences, and genetics shape who you are, but they do not have to define you." I tell them very clearly, "You are the CEO of You, Inc. If you want different, you can have different, but you have to do different. Take control!"

I got into this business because I began to think about my legacy and wanted to do something that would last and change lives. I recognized very early on that we're only here on earth for a very short period of time. I wanted to make it a meaningful, lasting impression for good.

My story begins a long time ago. We lived in a poor neighborhood. My mother worked in a factory for $1 an hour. We were poor.

Like other women who worked in factories at that time, my mother experienced many instances of sexual harassment. She became an activist, one part Norma Rae and one part Coal Miner's Daughter. It wasn't safe for groups of women to gather openly during the day, so she would invite them to our home after dark. The women were a diverse group of African-American, Latina, and white women. They were all poor, trying to make ends meet with a low-paying factory job.

My mother thought I was asleep when she held these meetings, but I would sit on the top stair and listen. My mother talked to the women and explained that they didn't need to give up and that the union (the Teamsters in this case) was behind them.

She would say, "When I get on top of those machines, and I say shut it down – Shut it down!" And the women would.

She said, "Don't worry about it! We'll shut it down. And the Teamsters will be there when I say shut it down. We've got the muscle right outside." And the muscle was there, and the management of the factory backed off.

But that didn't make everything easier. If we went out to dinner at night, we'd need to have "muscle" protecting us all the time. Once, and I'll never forget this, a firebomb was thrown through our front window. And we all just got up and got the little fire taken care of.

It was after that firebomb that my mother sat me down. She had tears in her eyes. She said, "Roger, you know, I love you with all my heart. I would do absolutely anything for you. But, honey, sometimes you just have to stand up for what you believe in because if you don't stand up, life will knock you down. And this is worth standing up for, not only for you and for me, but for every mother that comes along after me that has to suffer like I've had to suffer to get you where you are and provide for you. But just know that I always love you."

She touched my heart. We got through it all. My mother has passed now, which is why I dedicate this book to her. I promised her I would never forget. There are still too many people who need help, and we can do it. I have long thought of the low levels of academic performance in our country as the civil rights issue of today. As I think about it more deeply, it has risen to the level of being a national security threat.

And to me, the greatest sin in the world is to let a child

suffer needlessly. If I can have a hand in helping children, I'm going to do it. That's what drives my life commitment of doing meaningful work for lasting good.

My daily prayer – the first thing I say in the morning and the last thing I say at night – captures this commitment. "Any kindness or any good I can do for any human being, let me do it now. Let me not defer nor neglect it, for I shall pass this way but once, dear God."

A Message from Betsy Hill

When I was a little girl, I had to wear glasses because my eyes didn't focus together. One ophthalmologist wanted to do surgery. But it would be cosmetic and wouldn't actually fix my vision problem. Another ophthalmologist, Dr. Margaret Gerber, who would end up becoming quite a leader in the field, recommended vision therapy. I went through childhood being taken out of school once a week for vision therapy sessions. Sometimes I had a patch of brown paper glued to the lens of my glasses, alternating which eye was covered to help strengthen the unrestricted eye. I was reminded daily to do my home eye exercises.

As my eyes improved a little, one exercise was to read without my glasses. I loved to read, so I hated to read without my glasses because it slowed me down. But one Saturday morning, I will never forget. I was sitting in the living room reading *The Five Little Peppers Midway* (emotion creates strong memories!). My mother reminded me to take my glasses off, making everything blurry, including the words on the page.

I read for a while, and then, all of a sudden, the print jumped off the page at me and became crystal clear. I was excited but terrified. At first, I didn't want to move, afraid it would go away, so I sat there, holding very still for a while.

Eventually, I looked around the room. For the first time in my life that I could ever remember, everything was perfectly clear, as if I still had my glasses on. I used to call it my little miracle. I now know that this is what happens when your brain works and works and works at something until it finally connects in just the right way to do something we don't have conscious control over. My passion and commitment started with having a personal experience in how the brain can change.

The second experience in my life that brought me to BrainWare was being a teacher. I went into teaching with all the enthusiasm and energy of any new teacher. I was committed to ensuring that all my students learned – in my case, foreign languages at the high-school level. It didn't work that way. I had studied the psychology of language, the philosophy of language, and linguistics, searching for some basis for understanding how our brains manage language. At the time, there was no science of language. Today there is, although there is still much to learn.

I have now taught at the elementary, middle, high-school, college and graduate levels. And it became clear to me that my repertoire of tools to help students who struggled was woefully inadequate back in my early teaching days. If I knew then what I know today, my teaching experience would have been quite different. Now, I have the opportunity to change that for teachers and students and their parents.

And the third experience that informs what I do today is that I raised three boys. I always say that if they hadn't been brothers, they never would have known each other. Same gene pool, same support and environment from the point of view of education – dramatically different learners. One scored at the post-high-school level in language in the fifth grade but took weeks of intense practice to learn to ride a two-wheel bike without falling into the bushes. One had extraordinary rhythm (later winning DJ competitions) but couldn't remember to turn his homework in. And one grasped math concepts like lollipops but was a minimalist when it came to written assignments.

When I first met Roger and BrainWare SAFARI, I was intrigued. It was plausible to me that cognitive skills could be developed. But I was skeptical. I am a data person. When the results from the first study were available, they were remarkable. Students experienced an average of four years, three months of cognitive growth in twelve weeks, and almost two years of growth on academic tests. Wow! Almost too good to be true, but I knew how the research had been conducted, so the evidence was there. And now I've seen it over and over again. Not only have I seen the research replicated with the same results, but I've also been fortunate to see the impact and hear the stories about the effects on individual lives.

Today, my mission is to help parents and teachers use the science of learning to improve academic and life outcomes.

Over the last fifteen years, Betsy and Roger have worked with schools, learning specialists, parents, and clinicians worldwide. They've touched lives in some seventy-one countries. They came to realize that those who are successful in changing their children's academic outcomes and developing their students' learning capacity had some important things in common. And the things they had in common often defied conventional wisdom.

Roger and Betsy developed and are ready to share the five simple steps parents take to help their children overcome learning struggles and become capable and confident learners. The simple steps that transform a child's learning capacity. The five simple steps that transform meltdowns into breakthroughs.

Let's get started.

CHAPTER ONE

The 5 Steps to New Hope for Struggling Learners

"Hi, I'm Marina. After using BrainWare SAFARI for twenty-seven weeks, I can say that it helped me to improve my spelling and do better at school. It built up my confidence to do my schoolwork on my own."

"Hi, we are the parents of Marina. We think the program is beneficial for everybody. We really enjoyed seeing Marina's progress with her cognitive skills clearly reflected in her academic work. We also found the program very useful for us, adults in our forties. It helped us to improve our memory skills and other cognitive skills."

—Raquel and Adrian M., parents of Marina (age thirteen)

The Lessons of Education from the Time of COVID-19

Many, if not most, parents have always assumed that the school system was responsible for educating their child. After all, that's where a big chunk of their tax dollars go. Over the last few years, we've seen more parents beginning to question that assumption. For the 35 percent or so of students who are performing proficiently at grade level in our country, maybe things have been working okay. But for the majority, for the 65 percent of students who aren't performing proficiently at grade level, the system hasn't been working. And nothing has made that clearer than families' experiences during the pandemic.

Remote learning has been an eye-opening experience for parents. Watching firsthand as their children struggled to stay focused and complete their schoolwork revealed some uncomfortable truths. We typically hear one of two things from parents.

"Wow! I never really appreciated how difficult my child is to teach. Now I have a far greater appreciation for what my child's teacher has to put up with. I don't know how the school does it."

Or ...

"Wow! I had no idea my child was struggling like this. They kept telling me everything was fine. My child was doing just fine, or so I thought. No problems? I feel like I've been lied to. It's obvious my child is struggling. And the school has done nothing! They just tried to keep me from seeing what I see now. I'm mad."

COVID-19 touched all of us. For many of us as adults, we just put our heads down and waited it out. We told ourselves that things would be strange for a few years, but we believed that our lives would return to normal at some point. As big a deal as it was, a few years in a young child's life is a much bigger deal.

The emotional toll was high for children unable to socialize with friends. For the children who had never been to school without a mask. And for the children who got no schooling at all, as happened in at least one school district for three months in the spring of 2020. Their rationale was equity. Apparently, no education at all seemed more equitable to that group of educators than pivoting to the models that others adopted.

The toll on learning has been devastating. True, remote learning helped some students, such as those who suffered from bullying at school, and some students actually did better learning remotely with fewer distractions or the ability to learn at a faster or slower pace. But the impact of COVID and remote learning on the education of many students – especially struggling learners – was disastrous and anything but equitable.

Just about every parent has worried. How can my child gain back the learning that didn't happen during COVID? And how can they do that when more learning slips away every week? Has the global pandemic stolen their childhood?

Schools were in and out of remote learning models across the country at different times. Initially, most schools moved to some type of remote learning, although there were also some that were able to preserve in-classroom (also called face-to-face) instruction. As restrictions loosened and schools started to return to in-person learning, some families were not ready to send their children back to the classroom. During the 2020-2021 school year, hybrid models were common. Hybrid models saw students splitting time between being online and being physically in the classroom. As the situation evolved in the spring of 2021, while many students were back in classrooms, some elected to stay remote. Then teachers had to simultaneously manage both models. And while it appears that schools are open again and students are physically in classrooms, too much has changed for us to really call it "normal."

By the fall of 2021, all public-school students were attending schools in districts that offered fully in-person instruction, according to Burbio, a data service that aggregates school calendars. And over 90 percent of students who took their beginning-of-year math and reading assessments through Curriculum Associates (i-Ready), did so in school buildings, rather than remotely.

An analysis of the data from beginning-of-year assessments by consulting firm McKinsey & Company,[1] indicated that:

- Students were about 3.5 months behind in math on average.

- Students were about 3 months behind in reading on average.

- Students of color and lower-income students lagged significantly more.

- Students with learning disabilities and English language learners were hardest hit.

One of the reasons for this disparity could be the different impact of remote learning. What just about any parent with a struggling learner can tell you is that their child didn't get the supports they needed during remote learning. Findings from a survey conducted by ParentsTogether[2] were striking.

---

1   Emma Dorn, Bryan Hancock, Jimmy Sarakatsannis, and Ellen Viruleg, "COVID-19 and education: An emerging K-shaped recovery," McKinsey & Company, December 2021, https://www.mckinsey.com/industries/education/our-insights/covid-19-and-education-an-emerging-k-shaped-recovery

2   ParentsTogther Action. "ParentsTogether Survey Reveals Remote Learning is Failing Our Most Vulnerable Students," accessed August 3, 2022, https://parentstogetheraction.org/2020/05/27/parentstogether-survey-reveals-remote-learning-is-failing-our-most-vulnerable-students-2/.

Students with IEPs Fared Worse During Remote Learning

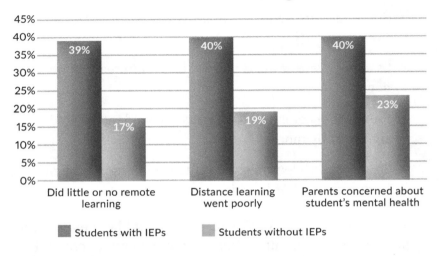

Figure 2. Students with IEPs (Individualized Education Plans) fared worse during remote learning.

The unfortunate truth is that the disparities that existed pre-COVID just got worse during COVID. Most children in the U.S. were not performing at grade level before COVID. And now, the kids who had trouble in school before are even farther behind.

As parents became more aware of their children's learning struggles and watched them try to do remote learning, some, like Monique Walker, responded by searching out a solution that would directly address their child's learning weaknesses.

"I felt the initial cognitive assessment process was very needed at the time. There were a few weaknesses that I knew Micah needed to strengthen. Micah's experience was very positive right from the beginning. I would have to say within the first week, I started to see a change. His coach was a perfect match, and they got along great. When I saw Micah have such a great response, I knew he definitely would be getting something out of the program. He was excited, so that made me get excited, and he would come to me and say, 'Oh, well, we did this, and we did that,' and I could just tell he was excited about what he was learning.

"I saw progress in Micah's work. At that time, he was doing the virtual learning, and I could really tell that the BrainWare program was making a big difference. There was a huge change in his perspective on learning. He had a different attitude, more of a positive attitude, and once he knew that he was successful with the program, he was willing to just take on bigger challenges. He has a different sense of confidence as far as perhaps attacking a situation in a more positive way. Instead of moving away from a situation or moving away from a problem, he attacks it head-on, and he uses certain steps, I guess, within his mental capacity differently than before.

"After one session, I asked Micah, 'What are you getting out of the program, and how do you like it?' His specific words were, 'I understand things from a different perspective now.' That was the $1,000,000 response. And that meant the world to me. If I'm thinking differently, I'm going to act differently. I'm going to approach my work differently. And even on a personal level, it just took him out of the box of his regular standard way of thinking or approaching a situation. I was so excited for him and so happy for him. And it helps from the mental health perspective. For kids, it's really serious now, you know, from just the day-to-day things they have to go through, and it has helped Micah go from internal to external. I don't have to bribe things out of him like I used to. I'm getting more than just a one-word response; I'm getting a paragraph. I'm getting him engaging in conversation."

—Monique Walker, mother of Micah (age fifteen)

Closing the COVID Learning Gap

To many, the solution to the learning gap was simply to open schools up again. To us, simply opening schools up again didn't address the learning gap because it treated it as if it were a teaching gap. Most of the early choices that schools have made on how to use emergency relief dollars – extended learning time, tutoring and assessments, remote learning technology – also treat the learning gap as if it were a teaching gap. And they don't address our children's capacity for learning.

In an online response to one of our posts on this topic, a teacher, Mona Ward, explained the problem this way:

"Children were one, two, three, four, and five grades behind before the pandemic, and nothing was done. Reopening the schools is happening, and children are still behind. So, eyes must be opened to truly understand that the district and school processes are failing students in all public schools.

"Teachers are implementing structures given by people over them. We are limited in our capacity to implement what we learned in college to do to educate individual children with different needs. So, just opening schools is not enough. Parents need to ask their child's teacher what they need to do to change an educational system so that education can really be about all children.

"When I first entered teaching, I could guarantee that my students would be 85 to 100 percent [performing at grade level] because I had an administrator who was not political and did not adapt initiatives to window dress his school. I could be creative and be out of the box and use all my degrees to enhance my students. Now, I implement plans that do not fit the individual needs of my students and am forced to analyze skewed testing data from three sources that each say something different for each child.

"This is not working for the good of students, and we have no buy-in regarding the adapting of initiatives that throw off a plethora of extra work for teachers that decreases teacher's time to plan for instruction. Did you know that teachers are charged to serve all their children in the classroom through a process called RTI [Response to Intervention]? This mandates that a teacher spend thirty to forty-five minutes on everything that a child scores low in, according to a test score.

"A teacher can't differentiate learning when almost every child needs an RTI in the general setting. There are few students prepared for school and who are at and above grade level. Please help transform schools not just to be open, but open to really serve children appropriately with 'just right' processes that promote learning."

—Mona Ward, teacher

The pandemic has made the flaws in our school systems more obvious, filled with mandates that provide more instruction but don't address the processes that "promote learning."

What would schools do differently if everyone thought about this as a learning gap, not a teaching gap? This may sound like an odd question because we've been speaking about learning gaps and learning loss and how students are behind. But many of the estimates of learning loss were based on how many days of school were being missed. And most of the "solutions" that are discussed are based on providing more teaching, such as tutoring, or one-on-one, intensive instructional academies. To a large degree, this is still looked at as a teaching gap.

If it's not a teaching gap, what is it? Here's the answer as explained by the Kennedy Forum[3]:

"Neuroscience research now proves what parents have known all along. Even the best teaching and curricula have surprisingly little effect when a child's cognitive and emotional readiness to learn is not addressed."

---

3 Kennedy Forum. Promoting Brain Health and Brain Fitness: A National Call for Action, Brain Fitness Brief, 2015.

The gap is a cognitive and emotional readiness gap, not an instructional gap. What this statement expresses so clearly is the importance of what each child brings with them to the learning process – emotionally and cognitively – and how that enables or stymies the impact of teaching and curriculum.

The pandemic has created an even greater crisis. And this crisis cannot be addressed by the same old approaches, like requiring teachers to teach and reteach the same material when students didn't get it the first time.

 **PARENT KEY 2**

Learning is what matters. Always focus on learning, not on teaching, accommodations or anything else. It doesn't matter how much teaching is going on if learning isn't happening. Too often, education focuses on "the what" (all the things we want children to know) rather than "the how" (how learning happens and how we can help students learn better).

Addressing Children's Cognitive Readiness to Learn

Curtis Boehmer was a speech and language pathologist in the Huron Intermediate School District working with students in Harbor Beach, Michigan. As a thirty-year veteran of helping students in the district, he decided to see if he could find any new brain research to help him with his struggling students.

His Internet search led him to BrainWare SAFARI, software that builds cognitive skills. The information he found showed that students who used the program for twelve weeks improved their cognitive skills by four years and three months. Their performance on reading and math tests improved by one year and eleven months.

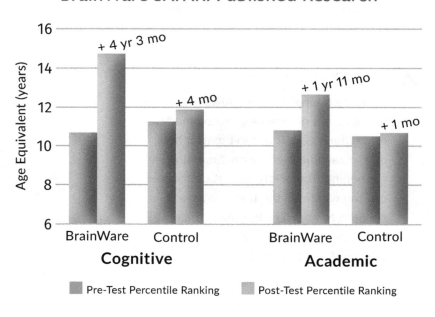

Figure 3. Cognitive and academic gains following cognitive training with BrainWare SAFARI.[4]

---

4   Don Helms and Sara M. Sawtelle, "A Study of the Effectiveness of Cognitive Skill Therapy Delivered in a Video-Game Format," Optometry and Vision Development, 38:1, 2007.

Curtis was intrigued but skeptical since he had never seen anything that could improve cognitive skills so dramatically in such a short time.

Curtis said, "You can't really believe everything you read on the Internet because anybody can type something up and put it out there. We looked at it, and all of us had the same comment – we've never seen anything that would change cognitive skill levels so dramatically and in three short months. Part of my training and services has been with severely cognitively impaired and moderately cognitively impaired students in our county. I just thought this is absolutely amazing. But we said, you know if it's there, they must be willing to put their reputation on it. And so, what we decided to do is run a ten-student study."

A BRAINWARE TEST STUDY

The district asked teachers to nominate students in second through eighth grades who might benefit from developing their cognitive skills. They randomly chose ten students to use BrainWare SAFARI after school for twelve weeks. Just as in the study that Curtis had found so amazing, the students experienced dramatic growth in their cognitive skills. In fact, their scores improved for their intellectual age by over three years ahead on the cognitive skills test Curtis gave them, after just 10 weeks of working in BrainWare SAFARI, and each and every student improved.

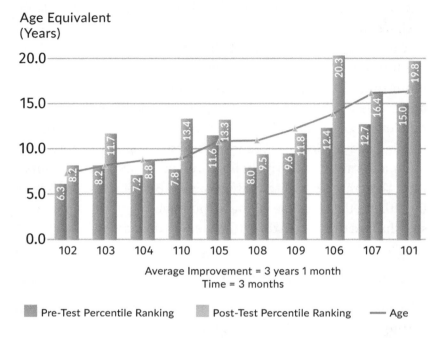

Cognitive Age by Student

Figure 4. Individual student cognitive growth, measured by Woodcock-Johnson Cognitive Battery, Harbor Beach, MI.

Curtis said: "I chatted with the teachers every single week about their students. I asked how school was coming. 'They're still doing the same thing. I'm not seeing anything different.' I got that comment from one teacher on a Monday about six or seven weeks into BrainWare. The next day, she actually came to me. I think that my question had just bugged her enough that she had gone home that night and sat down to really look at how that student was doing in class. She came to me, and she said, 'You know what, Curtis? I haven't even noticed. Still, his whole performance is just slowly rising. It's gradual.' There weren't giant leaps in performance in the classroom over those first six or seven weeks. Still, they were slowly rising, and it was starting to increase. And she was just absolutely floored.

"I started having teachers ask to stop by after school and see what was going on. They wanted to know what we were doing because they really didn't understand it. But they knew something was happening with their students. So, we invited them to sit in with their student. Their students showed them what they were doing. When the teachers tried to help their students, the kids insisted, 'I have to do this on my own, and you just get to watch.' And so they did.

"I had a science teacher come down and want to know what we were doing. He said, 'Curtis, tell me what this student is doing down here because I think he cheated on the test he just took. This kid has never gotten a grade like this before.' And I suggested, 'Well, you know what? You have to look back at his daily work recently. What's his daily work like? And talk to him and find out. Take a look at his notebook to see where his notes are at.'"

Curtis and the science teacher (we'll call him Mr. Smith) talked to the student and asked him what he had done differently. "I dunno," he said, as students typically do. "Well," he said. "I did take notes." Now it would be easy to stop there. Of course, a student will do a better job studying if they actually take notes. But there was more. "I never was able to take notes before. Mr. Smith used to talk so fast I couldn't keep up. I couldn't take notes and follow what he was saying at the same time. Now he talks slower." Both Curtis and Mr. Smith knew that Mr. Smith hadn't suddenly slowed down. He had been teaching science for thirty years. What had happened is that this student's cognitive skills were now stronger, and he was able to do the complex tasks of listening and taking notes at the same time. His brain was able to keep up with the pace and demands of the class.

Curtis said: "And there was a change in actual classroom behavior, too. This student wasn't a huge behavior problem before BrainWare. Still, he certainly had his issues in class that disturbed the classroom and the teacher. We're talking about a pretty smart kid that just didn't get school, and he changed his behavior. His behavior was more acceptable in class. The amount of time the teacher focused on behavior with him was reduced because of his academic performance. It's going to make the teacher's job easier, and they're going to be able to cover their math or science better and go more in-depth. The students will respond better because they will take what they learned in math, science, and language arts and use it in their other subjects."

 **PARENT KEY 3**

Learning happens inside your child's brain. And every brain needs to be ready for learning. The skills that form the foundation of learning are called "cognitive skills." Cognitive skills are the processes our brains use to take in, understand, store, retrieve and apply information from the outside world. Cognitive skills are how we learn.

The Old Approach

Many of you are probably familiar with the old approach to helping students who are having difficulty in school. The old approach starts with reteaching the material that a student didn't understand the first time. And reteaching and reteaching and reteaching. That's the approach described by Mona Ward, the teacher quoted previously. When that doesn't work, the other elements of the old approach include:

1. **Accommodations** (for example, giving a student extra time to finish a test).

2. **Modifications** (for example, a student is graded on a lower scale than their peers or reads a text at an easier level).

3. **Compensatory strategies** (for example, a student with limited working memory receives written or oral instructions one step at a time).

These adjustments don't try to make the child's learning processes stronger for their future. The purpose is to help students avoid their areas of weakness.

The New Approach

The new approach doesn't help students avoid their weaker cognitive skills. It actually helps develop cognitive skills so that they can use them to learn more efficiently and effectively. Today, we know that cognitive skills can improve, often more than anyone thought.

"I spent the better part of my years in grammar school in LD [learning disabled] classes, where I wasn't challenged. I suffered when I made the transition to "mainstream" classes. My performance was average at best, but I was able to teach myself the necessary skills to be as successful as my peers, and did the same at all of the subsequent transitions to junior high, high school, college and graduate school. After having worked through BrainWare SAFARI, I can attest to its usability as well as playability. Had I been given such a tool in my early stages of learning, I believe my time in school would have been less difficult."

—Joshua Woodward, MSW, Chicago, IL

 PARENT KEY 4

Cognitive skills can be developed to a greater degree than most of us realize. If you and your child are told that they have a weakness in one or more cognitive skills, it is not a life sentence. These are skills that can be strengthened and trained to work better and in a more integrated way.

Students Who Learn Differently

"Before BrainWare SAFARI, Adam used to drift away a lot and get distracted when he was doing challenging problems, especially in math. Now he's more focused. We're really pleased with that. It's a wonderful program."

—Harlan K., father of Adam (age twelve)

The families that we work with talk about their children's learning issues in a variety of ways. Some children have a diagnosis, like attention deficit (hyperactivity) disorder (ADD or ADHD), autism (ASD), dyslexia, nonverbal learning disability (and many others). But many do not. They may just have difficulty with reading comprehension or math, getting started on their homework, remembering information from one day to the next, processing speed or staying focused. The fact of the matter is that each of these children simply learns differently.

Diagnoses like ADHD and autism are not actually all that helpful in supporting a child in learning. This is because cognitive skills are highly variable across students, even within a single diagnosis. And kids without a formal diagnosis also have cognitive strengths and weaknesses. Indeed, we all have cognitive strengths and weaknesses. What a parent needs to understand and what BrainWare programs help with is understanding how children learn differently.

When it comes to helping students overcome learning challenges, there is the old way and the new way. The old way uses accommodations and adjustments to curriculum and instruction to enable students to work around their cognitive weaknesses. The new way builds weaker cognitive skills and areas that are already strong so that learning is more effective and efficient.

5 Simple Steps

We've worked with many thousands of parents, teachers, students, school administrators, clinicians and researchers over the years. In that time, we've seen both life-changing transformations and efforts to help children overcome learning struggles that fell short of the goal. We've learned a lot because we had to. There was no one who had traveled this road before.

Now that we've traveled the road and mapped the route, we know there's a process – 5 Simple Steps – that lead to success. These five steps help children overcome their struggles at school, turn their academic careers around, and build a solid foundation to be well-rounded, successful young adults with a comfortable sense of personal well-being.

The 5 Simple Steps our clients use to help their child overcome learning struggles are like a recipe. When you add the same ingredients in the same order, you get the results you are looking for – every time. The 5 Steps explicitly address the fact that every child learns differently.

Your child is unique. But they also have something in common with every other child whose parents have followed the 5 Steps – the fact that brains can change. The scientists call this neuroplasticity. Neuroplasticity simply means that brains can change. And the science is now clear – they can change way more than most people know. Whatever a child's learning strengths and weaknesses, they can be improved. It just takes careful attention to the steps we outline below and discuss in detail in the next five chapters of the book.

Following all of the 5 Steps is important. Don't think you can skip directly to Step 4 or 5. And don't stop part way through! If you take only four of the steps, perhaps you will see some changes, a little improvement here or there. But if you take all five steps, you will be among many successful parents and teachers watching a dramatic, positive change in your child.

The 5 Step system is like the favorite family recipe that you have grown to trust and rely on.

The 5 Simple Steps: The New Way, Not the Old Way

The steps are simple, and they reflect the new way of helping children overcome learning struggles. If you want different results than you've seen for your child in the past, then you have to think different, and you have to do different.

The 5 Steps are:

1. Take the Wheel

2. Set High Standards

3. Build the Cognitive Infrastructure for Learning

4. Move Beyond Grit

5. Invest in a Coach

STEP #1 – TAKE THE WHEEL

The first step to making a change is taking control. Most parents are used to leaving learning matters to their child's school. We will discuss how you can use the information your child's school gives you. But you can't stop there. Leaving everything to the school and just hoping for the best is not the answer. You need to take the wheel and drive to the future you want for your child. The old way is leaving it all to the school. The new way is to take the wheel.

STEP #2 – SET HIGH STANDARDS

Conventional wisdom says not to put too much pressure on kids who struggle with learning. You may have heard that and wondered if letting kids off the hook by changing the requirements for success is a good idea. Yes, we need to help kids who are anxious (and many kids with learning struggles also suffer from anxiety), but we don't need to lower our ultimate expectations for them. Lowering expectations will not do them any favors when they are grown. Accommodations and work-arounds may be needed in some cases, but the goal is to move ahead so your child can succeed beyond them. The old way is lowering expectations. The new way is setting high standards and providing kids with the tools to meet them.

STEP# 3 – BUILD THE COGNITIVE INFRASTRUCTURE FOR LEARNING

Here you will learn about the way brains work, in general, and your child's brain in particular. Every mind is unique, and there is some basic information that every parent should know about their child's brain. Discover what makes it easy for your sister to keep her closet organized. See how your best friend "just knew" the answer in math class. And uncover some of the mysteries that make it more difficult for your child to succeed in the classroom. The old way is hit or miss. The new way is understanding your child's learning strengths and weaknesses and helping them develop their learning capacity.

STEP #4 – MOVE BEYOND GRIT

So often, children are told by teachers (and parents) to "try harder." And perhaps sometimes that would make a difference. But mostly, when a student doesn't "try hard enough," there are underlying reasons. Students who are disorganized don't want to be disorganized. Kids with behavioral problems (in class and at home) don't get up in the morning planning to misbehave. Children who deal with anxiety or perfectionism or low self-esteem don't strive for that. They try hard but end up discouraged. The old way is telling kids just to work harder, to have more grit. The new way is explained in Chapter 5.

STEP #5 – INVEST IN A COACH

We've already mentioned cognitive training, and Chapter 6 will go in-depth on how comprehensive, integrated cognitive training works, why it makes a difference, who it helps and how a personal coach can help you and your child get the most out of the experience. This is what makes the process truly transformational. The old way is helping children work around their weaknesses. The new way is building strong learning skills for a lifetime.

So, let's get started looking at the 5 Simple Steps parents take to help their children overcome learning struggles and become capable, confident learners. And remember, if, at any time, you want to talk with Roger or Betsy, you can book a call at https://mybrainware.com/schedule/ or 877-BRAIN-10 (877-272-4610).

"Fourth grade was miserable for my daughter. Even though she did her homework every night and had a reading tutor, she wasn't able to retain facts, she read at a second-grade level, and she rarely passed tests in class. Her teacher requested holding her back.

"She started using BrainWare SAFARI two weeks before fifth grade. After just three weeks of practicing four to five times per week for thirty minutes each session, she was not only telling me her multiplication facts, but figuring out her division facts. Her reading comprehension has increased, and her ability to write paragraphs. This program has been a gift."

—A mother

CHAPTER TWO

Step #1   Take the Wheel

"I just want to take the time to say thank you for showing
me ways to help Roger and providing the resources that
we need for his academic growth. I took the information
to the IEP meeting, and it was the best IEP meeting that
I ever attended. I felt empowered because I knew the
terminology in a way to assist Roger to help him get
the support that he needs. His teacher was excited, and
the IEP team was happy for Roger and me. It was a very
productive meeting."

—Melissa B., mother of Roger (age ten)

◾ A Parent's Job

You probably believe, as we believe, that a parent's number
one job is to raise a positive, self-sustaining, proactive human
being who contributes to their immediate family and the community at large.

That can seem like a pretty tough assignment, especially
when you get to the bumps in the road. Early bumps in the
road like trying to figure out your baby's feeding schedule and
potty training usually pass fairly quickly, even if it doesn't seem
so at the time. But later problems, especially when kids get to
school age, may not be temporary inconveniences.

For many parents, and perhaps for you, school and learning
issues sound like this: "I just felt desperate. I wanted things to
be better for my son, but I didn't know what to do." We hear
this kind of statement over and over from parents.

Like most parents, you may doubt how prepared you are
for many of the problems you confront as a mom or dad. Most

of us don't get an advanced degree in parenting before we embark on parenthood. And many parents don't feel they have the answers when it comes to their child's education.

Here's what you really need to know. When it comes to how children learn, especially children who learn differently, educators don't have all the answers either. Most educators don't know what you will learn in this book.

The other thing to remember is that you are the one who cares about your child – more than anyone else in the entire world. At the end of the day, no one else has the love, the commitment or the power to help your child overcome their learning struggles.

And never, ever forget that your child is unique. They may share physical features with other family members. They may have personalities that are similar to other children. But no two individuals are truly identical, even identical twins!

Every brain develops uniquely. When it comes to learning, assuming that children all learn in the same way is like saying they all look the same or like the same foods. And you are the one who can ensure that your child gets the unique support and help they need to grow and thrive and fulfill your dreams for them and their dreams for themselves.

We get the pain and struggles that your child experiences every day. What we are striving for in this book is to bring clarity to what parents need to do to provide their child with the best opportunity for their dreams to come true. Whose dreams? The word "their" in the last sentences is ambiguous. It could refer to your dreams for your child or your children's dreams for themselves. We mean both. Do not let anyone steal your child's dreams or your dreams for them!

The issues you are dealing with are like a puzzle. If you are ever going to figure it out, you must start at the foundational level of your child's learning capacity. A lot of parents may not have realized that learning reading and math don't just "happen" automatically until their child didn't learn to read as other children did. Most parents don't even know that they need to be talking about skills that are even more basic than ABCs and 123s.

If you don't know about the role that cognitive skills play in learning, it's because most of the education system hasn't sorted this out either. But as we said earlier, the research is clear. Half of the difference between the academic performance level of a successful student and the academic performance level of an unsuccessful student is explained by their cognitive skills.

Cognitive capacity has by far the greatest impact on successful learning. Everything flows from a child's cognitive capacity. Cognitive capacity is the foundation, and we have to start there. If we don't, it's like watering the leaves of a tree rather than the roots. And as Alan Nishino, former superintendent of the Filmore Unified School District in California, once told us, "As educators, we spend all of our time watering the leaves. We need to be watering the roots."

So, taking the wheel means starting to understand how your child learns and why they are struggling with learning and schoolwork. And that process starts with a cognitive assessment. Okay, it's a test – a measurement. But it's a different kind of test than kids typically take in school. It won't tell us what grade level they're reading at. It won't tell us if they know their math facts. It WILL tell us what we really need to know – how they learn best.

Some of our clients have already been through a cognitive assessment with their children. Typically, the purpose of the assessment is to determine whether or not the child qualifies for services under the IDEA (Individuals with Disabilities Act). If the assessment leads to a diagnosis of a learning disability or ADHD or another disability listed in the law, they usually get an Individualized Education Plan or IEP. If the child has an IEP, they were probably tested with what is often called a neuropsychological evaluation. The results of most neuropsychological testing are not typically presented in a way that is meaningful to parents. Parents are told that their child does or does not qualify for services/supports, but that is often the extent of their understanding of the tests.

Our approach to a cognitive assessment is different.

First, the initial assessment results and consultation explain to parents what the results mean regarding the likely impact of a child's cognitive strengths and weaknesses on their school performance and what parents see at home.

PARENT KEY 5

Your child, like every other child, truly learns uniquely, with their own particular cognitive strengths and weaknesses. If you don't know what they are, no one can help them apply their strengths to master learning tasks that are challenging. And no one can provide just the right supports to facilitate learning and improved academic performance.

Second, the assessment results are used to develop an individualized learning plan for each and every student we work with. The plan guides us in the application of time and resources. There are thousands of evidence-based strategies for learning. But not every strategy works for every child. Many IEPs and other accommodations are not very individualized and often include the same kinds of supports, regardless of the student's needs. What we do is take the information from the assessment and use it to filter the most relevant strategies for a particular student. Then, one of our neuroeducators (an experienced educator with extensive training and experience in the application of neuroscience to learning and teaching) refines the strategies in consultation with the parents. The child's teacher may also be involved (and is always welcome). The plan accounts for the learning environment and the student together. This has been especially important during the many changes in what school has looked like starting with COVID.

We describe the assessment as a GPS for learning. It will tell us where your child's cognitive learning strengths are and where barriers are. From there, we can see where we are, where we need to go and how to get there. This is about having a clear road map that will clarify exactly where we need to begin to optimize their journey for life success.

And finally, and most importantly, the cognitive assessment serves as a baseline. This is the STARTING POINT. After our clients' children go through their cognitive training to enhance their underlying learning skills, we assess them again and can report their cognitive growth to their parents.

Why a Parent Notices First (Usually Mom)

If you notice that maybe your child is beginning to struggle in school, you may assume that the teachers are already aware of this. You may assume that they're going to just step in, figure out what's going on and make the changes needed. But the fact of the matter is it's probably you – the mom or the dad – who is going to notice it first. There is nobody who knows your child better than you do. You can see when they start to lose curiosity. You notice when they begin to lose the joy of learning. You are in the thick of it when they begin to avoid getting started on homework because they're not sure they can rise to the challenge.

You are the guardian of your child's learning. It may be that school can help, but it will likely be up to you to bring it up. And it will likely be up to you to make sure that the underlying reasons for their learning struggles are uncovered. When you know what those underlying reasons are, you can understand why it's happening, and they can be addressed.

"Since our children have been using BrainWare SAFARI, I have noticed that their memory and attention abilities were dynamically increased. We live abroad, and my children go to school in the host language. I feel that this program is significant in bolstering their ability to understand and problem solve, most particularly in difficult foreign-language learning situations. My children love the program. I can assure you that the activities stimulate their brains, and the activities themselves draw them back. I highly recommend this."

—Darlene B, mother of four, American abroad

Teachers and schools generally don't have the answers today for the 65 percent of students who are not performing proficiently at grade level. Schools can be very good at telling you what your child should learn and whether or not they've learned it. But they are not very good at explaining how your child learns and how the school supports your child's unique strengths and weaknesses.

Things didn't go so great when COVID-19 forced schools to close. Admittedly it wasn't easy for anyone. But school systems may be some of the least adaptive institutions in our society. When they tried to pivot, it was a major struggle. They got caught up in bureaucracy, conflicts with unions, conflicting and unreasonable demands from parents, lack of plans, technology and teacher training to shift to online learning. If we heard one story about schools dropping everything just to ensure that their students got fed, we heard hundreds. Priorities are priorities. And schools reverted, naturally, to the lowest levels of basic human needs, which Maslow's hierarchy reminds us are … food, shelter, clothing. It was necessary, but some important things got left behind – like our kids' education.

Who got left behind in the scramble? There is substantial evidence supporting what we observed with the families we work with – students who learn differently were disproportionately impacted academically by COVID-19.

"But I pay my taxes," you may say, as do many parents. Yes, you do. But the funding of education is disconnected from the process of learning.

Unfortunately, the truth is that most educators don't know how learning happens. Most teachers have not been trained in the neuroscience of learning. They don't know how information is processed in the brain. They don't know about the cognitive processes that are the foundation for learning. Great teachers embody in their teaching how learning happens but seldom because they have been taught about it. Most teachers don't know how to identify learning strengths and weaknesses and what to do about it if they do. And in most schools, they have few resources that would enable them to do either.

Understanding cognitive skills is where it starts. Where it ends is with a child who has become more capable and confident as a learner. And that end is just the beginning. This journey is a gift that will give for a lifetime. As a parent, you cannot always write the beginning of your child's story, but you can have a major impact on how your child's story ends.

If there is one thing for certain, God did not make any junk, and we assure you he did not start with your child!

"It's been a phenomenal experience to watch both children go through BrainWare SAFARI, especially Brianna. Brianna was having some challenges in school, and after she completed BrainWare SAFARI, she made the honor roll, which has been exciting and a very proud moment for me as a father."

—Patrick Tharp, father of Brianna (age eight)
and Angela (age ten)

■ Step #1 Is to Take the Wheel

Take the wheel. The cavalry is not coming. If your child is struggling, the odds are that their school will not have identified why they are struggling or done what is needed to help them get on track.

If you want different, you have to do different. And to do different, you have to think different. Like understanding the role of cognitive skills and the importance of determining your child's cognitive strengths and weaknesses.

A big part of your child's success will depend on your mindset. You have to own this process. You are the most important person in your child's life and are in a better position than anyone else to make change happen. If you don't, probably no one else will. And nothing will change.

When we meet parents, we often ask them where they got their Ph.D. in parenting. Right away, they look at us and kind of roll their eyes. We say, "Sure, one morning mom wakes up and says, guess what? We're going to have a baby!" Well, no one gets a Ph.D. in parenting. And like all parents, you don't know how to handle every single problem that you're confronted with as a parent. None of us does. And that is especially true when it comes to your child's education. If you are worried that you don't have what it takes, remember all the other things in life that you've done that you didn't know how to do until you decided to do them.

Raising a child can be a very daunting task these days. You'd think the internet would help, but sometimes there are just way too many options. Making choices among all the options the internet puts in front of you can be overwhelming – you only have so much time in the day. So, you likely feel like you don't have all the answers.

To be clear, some schools and educators address the full range of students that enter their classrooms. But that is not the case for the majority of students in this country. If schools really understood how to help all students succeed in learning, the national statistics wouldn't be what they are. We would have more than 35 percent of fourth graders reading proficiently at grade level. We would have more than just 41 percent able to do math proficiently. If schools knew what to do to help every child learn, the statistics would have become a lot better, but they aren't.

For the last half-century (since the 1960s), the educational policies of our country have been designed (or so we are told) to "level the playing field." Specifically, the goal has been to close the performance gap between populations that perform well on academic assessments and those that underperform year after year. Since the 1960s, when President Johnson decided to attack these challenges within our education system, we have spent $22 trillion of our tax money to try to change it. We'll be spending more money. And nothing has really changed for children who learn differently. In fact, the most recent evidence is that it has gotten worse. The National Center for Educational Statistics has reported that reading and math scores for fourth graders in 2022, following the pandemic, dropped to levels not seen in two decades. The report also reveals that lower-performing students' scores dropped more than those of higher-performing students.[5]

Either schools have no idea how to solve these challenges, or they're keeping it a secret. Frankly, we don't think they're keeping it a secret.

You don't have the answers yet either, but give yourself the credit you deserve. There are a lot of things you've come to do very effectively that you had no idea how to do before you started. We believe in you. If your child is struggling, you have the power to change it. It's not a hope. It's not a prayer. It's a promise from us. And we can promise this because we can empower you with the ability to directly affect the factors that account for half of your child's learning outcomes.

Remember, in the introduction, when we talked about the fact that cognitive skills explain 50 percent of academic performance? That's something you can do something about.

---

5   National Center for Education Statistics, NAEP Long-Term Trend Assessment Results: Reading and Mathematics, 2022, accessed at https://www.nationsreportcard.gov/highlights/ltt/2022/.

You may have no control over who your child's teacher is, what curriculum the school uses, how large the class is, or what technology there is. But those things account for less than half of the outcome. With the 5 Simple Steps in this book, you are the one who can actually take the wheel to help your child develop the skills that can lead to a lifetime of success – both personally and professionally.

"BrainWare has been wonderful for my son! He's fourteen and has really struggled with attention deficit, auditory processing, thinking and concentration. I am absolutely convinced that BrainWare has improved not only his ability to stay focused but his overall achievement. He's zooming through his regular assignments now, and I'm having to supplement with more challenging work to keep him engaged."

—Mary O., parent

■ Ask Yourself and Your Child's Teachers: What is learning?

How would you answer the question: What is learning? How do you think most educators would answer? Typically, the answers we hear when we ask that question relate to acquiring new knowledge or skills, being able to do something we couldn't do before, and the like. While those answers are true, it is not how we would answer the question.

Our Answer: Learning is the making and strengthening of connections among neurons into networks in the brain. Whoa! Yes, probably different from what you were thinking, but we'll break it down.

PARENT KEY 6

Learning is a biological process that involves a physical change in the brain. Learning is not about a teacher transmitting knowledge or pouring information into a student's brain. Learning is the process of each brain constructing its understanding of the world for itself.

Some teacher preparation programs are starting to include training on how the brain learns. Still, most teachers never heard the word "brain" in their education programs. And what is that all about? The brain is the organ that learns!!! As Leslie Hart, author of multiple books on the brain and learning, said,

> Education is discovering the brain, and that's about the best news there could be ... anyone who does not have a thorough, holistic grasp of the brain's architecture, purposes, and main ways of operating is as far behind the times as an automobile designer without a full understanding of engines.[6]

When we make statements about teachers' lack of understanding of the brain and how learning happens, it upsets many of them. They are offended. They protest that, of course,

---

6 Leslie A. Hart, *Human Brain and Human Learning* (Kent, WA: Books for Educators, 1999), p. xi.

they know how learning happens. But the evidence is that they mostly don't. So, when your child struggles in school, the responses are likely to be to reteach the same material in the same way (when they didn't get it in the first place) or to say that the student needs to work harder.

■ A Message from Dr. Pat Wolfe

Pat Wolfe is one of the pioneers of applying neuroscience research to classroom practice. In addition to authoring *Brain Matters: Translating Research into Classroom Practice*, she has trained thousands of administrators, school board members, parents and teachers across the United States and around the world. She has taught at all levels from kindergarten through college. She has served as the Director of Instruction for the Napa County Office of Instruction (Napa, CA) and was the lead trainer for the International Principal Training Center in Rome and London. As a consultant and trainer, she focused on the educational implications of neuroscience, cognitive science, and educational research for learning and teaching. She also conducts workshops on the brain and addiction, reading and the brain, early brain development, and the aging brain. Her message comes, in part, from testimony presented at a Joint Congressional Briefing on Neuroscience in the Classroom.[7]

---

7   Joint Congressional Briefing on Neuroscience in the Classroom, hosted by Learning Enhancement Corporation, in cooperation with U.S. Representative Danny K. Davis, Washington, DC, January 23, 2013, Transcript of Video Recording, https://youtu.be/UoeZCQIpgX0.

"Today we're looking at a new scientific foundation for the educational field. We've entered an information age with the potential for neuroscience to provide us with a much better understanding of learning. I think there are four major findings.

"Number one is called neuroplasticity. The brain is the only organ in the body that you change minute by minute by minute. It's malleable. You can change it. The brain you're born with is not the brain you're stuck with. For example, when a baby is born blind, the neurons in the visual system aren't working. What do you think is going to happen to those neurons that never get activated? You would think they would atrophy, but they don't; they change their function and become auditory neurons and tactile neurons. This is why people who are born blind have a better sense of hearing and tactile sensation. And new research shows that children who are born deaf have better peripheral vision. So the brain is changing on its own based on what it's experiencing.

"The second finding is that the brain is a pattern-seeking device. What that means is that if the information doesn't have any meaning to you – if you can't hook it to something you already know – it's gone. A friend of mine calls it educational bulimia. You just suck it up, regurgitate it on the test, and it's gone.

"The third one is that emotions play a much stronger role in learning than we have ever realized. We can tell that by looking at cortisol levels in the brain. When you are under strong stress, the frontal lobes of the brain shut down. The frontal lobes of the brain let you do your higher-level thinking and problem solving. When you are under stress, they shut down. If a student perceives the classroom or his or her peers or the teacher or parents to be threatening, they don't learn.

"The fourth one is that we have two very different types of memory. One type of memory is for things that have gotten to the level of automaticity. You don't have to think about walking, and that's good because if you had to decide which muscles to use, you'd never get very far. You've done it over and over and over until it's reached the point of automaticity. We call this procedural memory, and the way you practice is by doing it over and over and over in the same way. The other type of memory (semantic or declarative memory) is the memory for concepts, and you need very different strategies for teaching concepts.

"We are really standing on the threshold of an era where neuroscience brain research has the potential to make tremendous strides in teaching and learning. I'd love to go back and start over again with what I know now. I think how we use this information as a new foundation of science for how people learn is probably the most important question that we're facing today.

"I'm very excited about BrainWare SAFARI because it's probably the first program I've ever seen that really tackles the cognitive skills that I think kids need. Rather than teaching them a specific skill like how to write a paragraph or how to solve an equation – those are important skills – but there are all kinds of underlying cognitive skills you need to be able to do that. So it's like instead of getting at the foundation, we're trying to treat surface areas.

"Here is a program that takes what is neurologically competent, what we know about how brains work. It also takes what we know about motivation and success and develops it into an engaging program. It develops a whole slew of cognitive skills that kids can continue to use for the rest of their lives. And it helps them to get those skills at the automatic level, so they don't have to say, 'Let me see ... what do I do?' It comes naturally. The whole concept is called automaticity. It's when you do something over and over and over to the point where it becomes automatic.

"I'd like to see good problem-solving skills at the automatic level. I'd like to see good attention skills at the automatic level. When you say to kids, 'Pay attention!' you've got a lot of kids who try but don't know how to do it. They don't have the basic skills to pay attention. BrainWare can, without kids even knowing that they're working on attention, develop some of those skills.

"Other products are in a totally different category. They, for the most part, focus just on one particular skill memory, like auditory memory. Plus, I've tried some of them and found them boring. Since I work in the field, I figured I should try some out, so when people ask, "What do you think of this? What do you think of that?" I could answer. I also think some claims are being made by some other programs that are not justified. They say they can help all kids when it seems they can only help some. I see BrainWare help all my kids because of its scope."

■ How to Take the Wheel

Likely, you are now seeing that your child's school does not "have the wheel." As well-intentioned as your child's teachers are, they simply have insufficient training in how the brain learns. They can't identify your child's cognitive strengths and weaknesses, and they can't tell how to help your child develop stronger cognitive skills.

Taking the wheel is mostly a mindset. When you accept that the school system has failed your child and you must step back in, you have taken the wheel. That may seem overwhelming at first, but remember, you are taking BACK the wheel. When a nurse handed that newborn child to you at the very beginning, you took the wheel. You had the wheel when you held your child in your arms, as you encouraged them to take their first steps, as you responded to their babbling and their first words. You had the wheel as you helped them on and off the potty, so somehow, they no longer wear diapers today. You were clearly at the wheel when you read books at bedtime and attended countless preschool shows.

Then, you took the step you had known would come someday. You dropped that precious soul off at school on their first day of school. Whether the tears were theirs or yours, that was the day, on some level, that you handed over the wheel.

And although your child now goes to school every day or attends those Zoom meetings when learning is remote, your mindset makes all the difference. When you retake the wheel, everything changes. As the captain of your child's learning voyage, your child's school and the teachers are members of the crew. With the right information and support, you need no longer dread parent-teacher conferences. You are back in control. So, breathe deeply. Imagine retaking the wheel. And we'll move forward to see how the rest of the steps can help you and your child move forward for educational and professional success.

PARENT KEY 7

There may be a lot of people willing to help your child, but there is no one that cares more than you do. Whether you brought your child into the world or brought them into your family, the connection you have is unlike any other, and there is no one else that can fill your shoes.

"My son was having some memory retention challenges. So, I was researching executive functions when I found BrainWare Learning on Facebook. I called them, and it has been a wonderful experience for him. I've seen a lot of changes. His memory has really improved. Now when I ask him how his day was, he can recount everything that happened. I am very happy to see the improvement. Now when I send him to school, I know he will be okay, even when they challenge him. This is a life-changing experience for my son. It is the best investment I have ever done."

—Zipporah Koimburi, mother of Cephas (age nine)

CHAPTER THREE

Step #2
Set High Standards

"I noticed a difference in his schoolwork. When I went in to see his teacher, she told me how well he was maturing, how well he'd done in his classes, and how easy it was for him to make progress. She now has to keep up with him in his schoolwork. Before, he was slower and afraid to make decisions. Now he makes decisions for both of us. He likes BrainWare SAFARI. I love it!"

—Debra W., mother of Demar (age ten)

Why It Might Be Hard to Set High Standards

What we hear all too often from parents is that other people – teachers, doctors, family members – have told them not to expect too much from their child. Every time we hear it, our hearts break. Because it's just plain wrong.

The critical second step in the series of 5 Steps is to set high standards, to expect more, not less. This may sound contrary to what you have heard before, but this step is vital. As the parent of a struggling learner, you don't want to see your child struggling in school. Your instinct is to shelter them from pain and frustration. It's natural to want to protect your child.

Setting higher standards may seem difficult. After all, if they are struggling to accomplish something, why wouldn't we just give them something easier? Why not just lower the bar?

And schools often push parents to accept lower expectations. It makes their job easier, and they look more successful.

They'll be careful how they say it, and they will probably emphasize that they believe all children can learn, but they'll be lowering the bar all the same. They make accommodations and modify the work your child needs to do. They make the schoolwork easier and easier, lowering the standards believing that that is the only way for your child to "succeed."

One of the reasons it can seem hard to raise the bar is that today ⊠ in school and outside of school ⊠ people spend a lot of time on labels.

■ Labels

Many of the kids we work with have a label – ADHD, learning disability, dyslexia, autism…. Some have more than one. Many don't have a label, but their parents are worried.

ADHD (attention deficit hyperactivity disorder) is a very common label these days. It refers to a developmental condition associated with difficulty focusing (paying attention) and often with impulsivity. Close to 10 percent of the population between ages two and seventeen have been diagnosed with ADHD.

The important thing to understand about labels like ADHD is that they are used for two things: 1) as the basis for medical treatment and/or 2) to qualify a student for educational services in school. That is, a doctor's diagnosis of ADHD is what qualifies a child to receive ADHD medications. The diagnosis of a learning disability is what qualifies a child to receive certain kinds of support, like working with a reading interventionist, in school.

What most parents don't realize is that a label doesn't tell us almost anything about how a child learns! We'll say this again and put it in a parent key because it comes as a surprise to many parents.

PARENT KEY 8

Just knowing that a child has ADHD or is on the autism spectrum or has a learning disability doesn't tell us what we need to know about how they learn.

So, expectations set by these labels don't make sense, even when we suspect that one of these labels might apply. If labels don't sufficiently characterize how a child learns, we should not confine our expectations and set standards based on them.

Which leads to the other reason it can seem difficult to set high standards. And that is that most parents aren't aware of the tools that are available to help children improve their learning capacity. In fact, there are tools and programs that help students learn more efficiently and easily and strive for and meet with greater success. We aren't in any way suggesting higher expectations without the right kind of support. We wouldn't do that anymore than we would suggest throwing a child into the deep end of a swimming pool and hoping they'll figure out how to swim. High standards have to be paired with effective support. We'll address what it means to provide children with the tools that help them live up to higher standards later in the chapter and in the ones that follow.

■ Living Up to Expectations

"Children are apt to live up to what you believe of them."
—Lady Bird Johnson

Sometimes kids defy the odds and pursue something they want without much support or encouragement from parents and others. But support and setting expectations make it a lot more likely. And there's a lot of research to support that.

Here are two very fundamental truths about children. One, they want to please us. Two, they want to live up to our expectations. And when we set high expectations, children respond well. If you set lower expectations for your kids, you might think you're doing them a favor because you're creating an opportunity for them to succeed. But the truth of the matter is that they will never expect more of themselves. It actually undermines their confidence in their own ability to grow and rise to expectations.

Children whose parents have high expectations for their children's success (academic and otherwise) generally get higher grades, do better on standardized tests, stay in school longer, have better motivation toward school and are more resilient. In fact, there's even evidence that high parental expectations can reduce the impact of lower teacher expectations for academic achievement.

There are two reasons to set high expectations. One is that if you set the bar too low, your child will probably meet that bar when they could have achieved and learned much more. Without high expectations, kids may not feel capable and confident. When they see that you believe they can achieve something, then they are more likely to believe. And it means that you will ensure that they get what they need to rise to your shared expectations.

As Henry Ford said, *"Whether you think you can, or you think you can't – you're right."*

The other reason for setting high expectations is that it affects how you will engage with your child's learning challenges. Expectations and effective support have to go hand in hand. If you set high expectations but turn it into a test – let's see if you can do this – it's very different than setting those expectations and then encouraging and supporting them in accomplishing it.

"There are different ways of going about the same task. Brains work very differently. The majority of kids in our program have atypical development and come at things in a very skewed way. [Using BrainWare] unpacks the process and helps teachers identify what needs to be taught explicitly in order to provide a more efficient strategy."

—Donna Kennedy, Head of School, Gillen-Brewer School[8]

8   Eve Müller, Ph.D., "Neuroscience and Special Education," inForum Brief Policy Analysis, National Association of State Directors of Special Education (NASDSE), 2011, p. 9.

■ Even with an IEP

Many of you may have participated in an IEP meeting. For those who haven't, an IEP is an Individualized Education Plan. It is a formal document created to meet the legal requirements for educating children with disabilities. It defines the services, accommodations and supports the school and teacher will provide to a child. It also sets goals for academic and/or behavioral progress.

The fact of the matter is that every child should have an IEP because every child has their own unique strengths and weaknesses. But in most schools, IEPs are only provided after testing shows clearly that a child needs extra supports. Nationwide, about 13 percent of students have IEPs and are therefore classified as special education (as opposed to general education). Their education is supposed to be governed by the IEP.

While parents often work very hard to get their child an IEP because they aren't succeeding in the general education environment, few IEPs are genuinely individualized. Most IEPs that we see are written to address a diagnosis, like ADHD or autism. They focus on the symptoms that show up in reading or math but don't actually address a child's specific learning strengths and weaknesses. In fact, it is uncommon for IEPs to acknowledge a child's strengths or help build on them.

Too often, IEPs are more about process and compliance than about finding out what really will work for a child. There's a lot of jargon involved in the IEP process, which is driven by legal and regulatory requirements. It is not unusual for the process and compliance to be the focus, rather than the child. This can be frustrating for parents and for the teachers who really would like to focus on helping a child learn. There isn't room in this book for an extensive discussion, but parents should be familiar with some terminology.

Many school systems use a process called RTI, Response to Intervention, or MTSS, Multi-Tiered Systems of Support. RTI and MTSS are similar in many respects, although MTSS often includes both academic and behavioral issues, while RTI tends to focus on academic issues. The idea is that students are grouped into tiers (levels) based on their needs at a given moment in time. Tier 1 includes the students who are making progress as expected with general classroom instruction. Tier 2 provides extra support (usually some individualized attention and reteaching content or teaching it in a different way) for students who aren't getting something. Tier 3 provides specific interventions to help students for whom Tier 1 and Tier 2 haven't worked. And if Tier 3 doesn't work, the student is referred for an evaluation to see if they qualify for Special Ed. If they do, they get an IEP.

One thing an IEP almost always brings with it is a different set of expectations for academic progress. So, the accommodations and supports aren't designed to help a child achieve what is expected for proficient grade-level work. They are designed to keep a child making progress, even if that progress is just incremental.

PARENT KEY 9

The traditional approaches schools use for children with learning issues are accommodations (e.g., extra time), adjustments to the curriculum (e.g., fewer spelling words), and compensatory strategies (e.g., writing down a list of tasks). What these approaches do is help students work around weaker cognitive skills. They don't actually provide ways to strengthen those skills.

■ A Message from Dr. Sarah Avtzon

Dr. Sarah Avtzon[9] is Assistant Professor and chair of Daemen University's Brooklyn, New York Branch Campus Graduate Programs in Special Education. She holds MS.Ed. and Ed.S. degrees from Teachers College Columbia University and a Ph.D. from Walden University. She works extensively with pre-service special education teachers.

There are two premises that underlie my sense of urgency today. The first one is the importance of cognitive skills in the learning process. I believe that what we're doing today with the children who struggle in the classrooms is highly improvisational and based on a lot of trial and error when in fact, there is an increasing awareness of the connection between cognitive skills and learning performance.

Flanagan and Harrison [researchers in the field of cognitive assessment] say that "Educational interventions that address cognitive processing limitations may be key to improving performance in academic areas where learning difficulties are manifested."

I acknowledge that until the very recent past, we perhaps did not know better. Accommodations, modifications to the

---

9   Joint Congressional Briefing on Neuroscience in the Classroom, hosted by Learning Enhancement Corporation, in cooperation with U.S. Representative Danny K. Davis, Washington, DC, January 23, 2013, Transcript of Video Recording, https://youtu.be/UoeZCQlpgX0.

environment and curriculum, and good teaching. That is what we are still training our teachers to do in order to increase student performance.

Findings by scientists who study the brain and brain imaging continue to reaffirm that cognitive skill training works. As J Giedd [child psychiatrist and researcher in the field of brain development] et al. have said, future research should not focus on whether it works or not but on what does it work on and how well does it transfer to academics.

This is what really pushed me into my research, to find the answers myself. I sat and listened to too many controversies among educators and other professionals about whether we could actually empower parents and children. About whether there are any long-lasting effects and whether there could be a chance to close achievement gaps.

I looked at our statistics in the United States. Out of the 13.4 percent of children receiving special education, 5.2 percent were children with learning disabilities. That accounts for about 40 percent of the students who receive special education in the U.S. If we take a look at the reading process, we see that many key cognitive processes have been identified as necessary for a child to decode, to be fluent or to comprehend. Visualization, the directionality of text, being able to hold information for a moment and then manipulate it later once they're done reading the paragraph, then reading the next paragraph and putting it all together – that comprehension is happening thanks to those key foundational cognitive processes.

The 40 percent of special ed students in the U.S. who have learning disabilities are sitting out there with these weak cognitive processes. It's an exasperating experience for them and adds to that lack of self-assurance and the lack of persistence or desire to persist on task. I looked at our population of students with specific learning disabilities, and I asked myself, "is there a pattern?" Notwithstanding the enormous controversy I encountered when I wanted to conduct my experimental design study, I found through a meta-analysis that was put together that five cognitive processes have been found to be common areas of deficit for children with learning disabilities: Auditory Working Memory, Nonverbal Problem Solving, Long-Term Memory, Processing Speed and Executive Functions and Attention. Researchers agree that in order to minimize the gap for students who are struggling in a classroom and, in this case, children with SLD [Specific Learning Disabilities], we need to enable them to have an overall cognitive ability level in these areas.

I decided to work with BrainWare SAFARI because the program was founded on the premise that you can train the brain as a comprehensive unit as opposed to isolating skills. All those neural networks have to be connected. So, the questions I had were: A) Does cognitive skill training have any significant impact on cognitive performance? B) If it does, does it have a different impact on different cognitive processes? C) And the million-dollar question, does it have any impact on academic achievement?

Every time I look at the results from the study, it gives me the chills. Using BrainWare SAFARI had a significant impact on those students. Their cognitive skills scores improved from 60 percent proficiency to 89 percent, just a little less than the 90 percent proficiency score that we expect out of typically developing children. And that was just in twelve weeks. I will never forget the face of one little boy beaming as he said, "I did it, Miss Sarah, and I even beat the timer!"

Now in terms of academics, the group that used BrainWare SAFARI became 31 percent more proficient in reading and 28 percent more proficient in math at post-assessment. The control group became only 1 percent more proficient in reading and 4 percent more in math. Since then, they've been in the classroom. The teachers have reported that the children are finally happy to learn and be in the classroom because they themselves are aware that they have an increased capacity to learn. That, to me, means the world, as a mom and as an educator.

These are staggering results, and the implications are so clear. It all depends on how well we educate and empower our children. This is the how part. How do we get all those students with different cognitive strengths who receive the same instruction in the same school and sit next to each other to be ready to achieve at the same grade level expectations we have for them?

———————————

Unfortunately, most special education programs and most IEPs still don't actually focus on helping students catch up to grade level in the subjects in which they are behind.

Part of the IEP process involves periodic meetings of the child's support team together with the child's parents, to review the student's progress. One member of our team sat through numerous IEP meetings as a parent, continually hearing about the little bits of incremental progress her children could expect. She expected more. She expected her children to catch up and have an opportunity to develop their unique strengths. She knew they had unique strengths. It wasn't easy. She had to hang tough with the school folks, but it paid off.

But what the school could provide was only part of the answer. When Karen learned about cognitive training with BrainWare SAFARI, she realized that it could help her kids build and strengthen the cognitive skills they needed to tap into their learning potential. As they did, they found it easier to listen to the teacher and take notes at the same time, to organize their work and to retain what they learned.

Without Karen's firm hand at the wheel, it wouldn't have happened.

Karen is one example of thousands of parents who didn't settle for incremental growth and for lower standards but who insisted that their kids, with the right help, could excel. Karen helped her daughter strengthen her cognitive skills so that she could catch up in school; her daughter went on to complete a nursing degree. Her work touches many lives on a daily basis, and she is a model for what can happen when a parent sets high standards. Winston Churchill once so famously said, "Never give in and never give up." We live by those words, as do our clients.

"I'm happy with BrainWare, and I've watched Nick's progress. His attention is better. I think his memory is better too. But what I really notice is that I don't have to repeat myself 20 times to get him to do something."

—Julie B., mother of Nicholas (age nine)

Not Just Your Average Students

Now, it's time to delve into what it means to say that a child learns differently. As a parent of a child who learns differently, you likely already have a feeling for this. Your child just doesn't "get" some things the same way that others do. You may have found ways to help them "get" things through your own ingenuity and persistence. But even with ingenuity and persistence, learning is complicated. Most parents and most teachers don't know what we are going to share with you now.

When children learn differently, which basically every child does, it means that they are not average in some respect. While kids can be average, on average, they aren't average on their own. Each has unique learning strengths and weaknesses. In the next several pages, we'll take a closer look at how unaverage students can be and how much their intelligence and special talents can be developed.

Before we go further, we want to check in with you on your mindset. First, there are going to be some graphs and statistics in this section. We know that some parents and kids have a fixed mindset about math. But don't think about it as math. Try to push through for some additional insights, even if you are tempted to skip past the numbers because your previous mindset says, "you're not good at math." Think, "They could be talking about my kid." Second, this section is where we really talk about how much intelligence can be developed. Believing that intelligence can be developed is also a matter of mindset. If you are skeptical, that's fine with us. We were both skeptics too. The research has persuaded us and we're eager to share it with you.

Note that when we talk about intelligence, we do it from the perspective that it is not one single thing. There are many aspects of intelligence that we refer to as cognitive skills. So, when we say that intelligence can be improved, we are saying that cognitive skills can be improved.

 **PARENT KEY 10**

Intelligence is not one thing. There are many aspects of intelligence that we refer to as cognitive skills.

In mid-2021, we decided to look at data for sixty students who had most recently completed our comprehensive, integrated cognitive training program. We started with data from the nationally normed cognitive assessment the students took at the start of the program. Usually, we use the data, student by student, to understand their individual cognitive strengths and weaknesses. We wondered what averaging the scores of this group of sixty students on each area of the cognitive test would tell us.

The cognitive assessment we use has ten sub-tests. In the next chapter, we will discuss cognitive skills in more depth since some of these skills won't be familiar to most parents. You probably have a good intuitive sense for some, like attention and visual and verbal memory. For now, it is enough to know that this assessment shows each student's cognitive strengths and weaknesses in ten areas important for learning.

Perhaps the easiest way to understand a score on a cognitive test (or on any test, for that matter) is as a percentile. A percentile is a ranking and basically indicates how a student performed relative to all their peers who took the test. If a student scores at the 70th percentile, it means that they scored better than 70 percent of their peers. If a student scores at the 50th percentile, they are right in the middle of the pack.

Most students (two-thirds) have scores in the "Expected Range" (between the 17th and 84th percentiles). And half of the students in the Expected Range will fall into what we can consider the "Middle of the Expected Range." Students who score at the 70th percentile or higher ("High in the Expected Range" and better) will typically learn whatever they are asked to learn in school without significant adjustments to the curriculum and instruction. In the Middle of the Expected Range, students typically learn what they need to learn, with good instruction and some of the supports teachers usually can provide in a regular classroom setting or with a little extra tutoring or review. Students who score below the Middle of the Expected Range will be unlikely to experience academic success without personalized supports, interventions and improvement in their cognitive skills.

The chart below shows the average percentile score for this group of sixty students on each of the ten subtests. Notice that the average scores for all of the subtests except Processing Speed are in the Middle of the Expected Range. The students' average score for Processing Speed was well within the broader Expected Range, although it was a bit lower than for other cognitive skills.

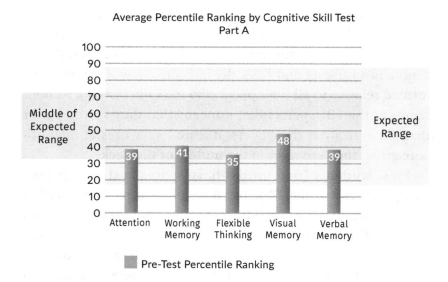

Average Pre-Test Cognitive Scores

Average Percentile Ranking by Cognitive Skill Test
Part A

Figures 5a and 5b. Average cognitive skills percentile rankings for sixty students.

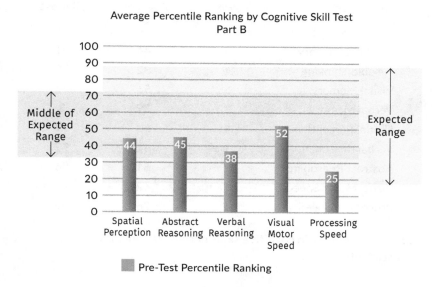

Figure 5b.

Are these just students with average learning skills who happen to struggle with academics?

Absolutely not!

What these averages don't reveal is the dramatic variability in individual student scores for these students.

Figure 6 shows the lowest percentile ranking for any of the sixty students for each skill, the average percentile ranking and the highest.

Test	Lowest	Average	Highest
Attention	1	46	84
Working Memory	6	44	81
Flexible Thinking	1	32	91
Visual Memory	5	56	93
Verbal Memory	1	39	3
Spatial Perception	1	50	99
Verbal Reasoning	1	41	99
Abstract Reasoning	7	51	96
Visual Motor Speed	1	62	96
Processing Speed	1	26	69

Figure 6. Variability in cognitive skills percentile rankings for sixty students.

In other words, in a sample of sixty students who have in common only that they struggle with learning and their parents sought our help, their scores were all over the board. Half of the students had a test score in the bottom 5 percent – we call that an exceptional weakness. But one-quarter of them had at least one skill in the top 5 percent. We call that an exceptional strength, and it is also often referred to as gifted. All of the students had cognitive areas that were above average and below average.

Not just your average students!

Before they saw the results of their child's cognitive assessment, these children's parents didn't know about their strengths, for the most part. They could see their children's struggles, but not where they were capable of really shining. Now that they could clearly see their strengths and weaknesses, they started to feel hope that if the children received help to improve some of the areas they struggled in the most, it could change how they experienced school and many everyday activities.

■ Some Thoughts on Learner Variability

Schools are paying more attention these days to the differences between learners and the need to adapt instruction. Differentiation and personalization are terms you might hear educators use when they refer to adjusting an assignment or instruction for different students. Just as important, though, is understanding what we can call "intra-learner variability." This type of variability is what is so obvious for the sixty students we have just been discussing. These students have very unevenly developed learning skills – with strengths, weaknesses and everything in between. This type of variability can be very puzzling and even frustrating, especially for the learners involved.

It is easy to oversimplify what students bring to the learning process. This is an A student. There is a B student. One is a strong learner. Another is a weak learner. He is bright. She is slow. They are lagging, etc.

Few learners are that consistent.

In *The End of Average,* Todd Rose[10] brings home the idea that each individual brings strengths and weaknesses to every academic experience (and, indeed, every life experience). If a student has strong perceptual skills and weak memory skills, their experiences in the classroom will be very different from a student with weak perceptual skills and strong memory skills. But it may not be obvious why because usually no one has measured these skills for each student.

---

10 Todd Rose, *The End of Average; Unlocking Our Potential by Embracing What Makes Us Different* (New York: HarperOne, 2015).

In fact, uneven cognitive skills can be just as stressful, sometimes more so, for a student than having more consistent but less strong learning skills. At this point, you might want to pause and review the list of cognitive skills in Appendix 1. Most likely you can identify skills that are probably stronger or weaker for your child (or for yourself).

When a student has really strong skills in some areas and weaknesses in others but doesn't know what they are or what the likely impact is, some learning experiences are easy, and some are difficult. But the student usually can't predict which will be which! Inexplicably, some things will be easy, and some will be hard. Some types of math problems will be obvious, and others totally obtuse (pun intended). Some language tasks will be super hard, but others will flow like the rain off a duck's back.

Students with highly variable learning skills typically experience a lot of frustration and anxiety. Teachers and parents may tell them, "Come on, you're so smart. You should get this."

Anxiety ...

Let's talk for a moment about anxiety. As parents and teachers, we can tend to dismiss the seriousness of the condition because we know it is a reaction to a possible future event, not something that actually exists. However, our bodies experience the same symptoms – our hearts racing, sweating and feelings of panic – with anxiety as with a currently present threat. Learning difficulties can lead to anxiety, and anxiety can exacerbate learning difficulties. Children with learning differences are far more likely to suffer from anxiety and, when that anxiety persists over time, they experience the chronic effects of stress. The relationship between learning issues and mental health issues is a close one.

Let's take one cognitive skill as an example – cognitive

flexibility (or flexible thinking). This skill is essential in determining when we need to change our approach to a problem but also in shifting between mental processes.

Say you have a student who reads amazingly fluently but stumbles when they come to a word they have never seen. And who can power through any math problem you give them until they get to one where all the operations and approaches they have learned don't apply. For this student, these challenges will probably seem "unfair," "frustrating," or even "impossible." They are used to succeeding in most reading situations and most math situations, but suddenly they feel stuck. They will likely be embarrassed, feel anxious, and it would not be surprising if they refused to continue reading and gave up on that math problem.

For this student, there is a common underlying cognitive processing reason for the difficulty they are experiencing in both subjects – less well-developed cognitive flexibility. However, most students (and teachers and parents) have the idea that reading and math are two different things. So, it is not obvious to the student – nor to their teachers – and that often causes them to doubt their ability altogether. Every learning situation brings uncertainty and, therefore, stress. Success seems like a matter of luck rather than something to which effort and strategies can be applied.

Now imagine that this student can be helped to understand the relative weakness of their cognitive flexibility (compared to memory, attention, and reasoning skills). Imagine that this student now has tools to strengthen their cognitive flexibility and strategies to compensate while they are building weaker skills.

Now learning situations will be less unpredictable and certainly less stressful. And talk about students taking responsibility for their own learning!

Figuring Out How Kids Learn Differently

"We just reviewed the report, and it was right on target. We reviewed it with our daughter, and she agreed with the weakness area examples. She even gave us examples of things that happened at school recently that we didn't realize. Even the aspects of her learning that we knew about generally. It was nice to put a name to it and get a detailed description of how it impacts learning. Our daughter was very excited by the resource recommendations."

—Father of a ten-year-old gifted girl

Sometimes people ask us about the profile of the students we work with and who benefits from cognitive training and assessment. We always emphasize that every child learns differently and has different cognitive strengths and weaknesses. There is no single common factor except that the student struggles in some way with learning. That should be evident from the "average" data presented above.

It can be confusing for parents not to know if their child is an "ideal candidate" for the program. That is completely understandable. Most parents don't understand what a complex and integrated business cognitive functioning is. Learning capacity is many things, and like weak links in a chain, weak cognitive skills can be the breaking point in a learning process.

We work with students with ADHD, autism, speech issues, vision issues, anxiety, dyslexia (trouble reading), dyscalculia (trouble doing math), dysgraphia (trouble writing), nonverbal learning disability, and students without any formal diagnoses or any identified learning disabilities. None of those labels captures the puzzle of each student's cognitive profile and where their strengths and stumbling blocks lie.

 **PARENT KEY 11**

A label may indicate that a child learns differently but not what their cognitive strengths and weaknesses are. And the absence of a label means nothing whatsoever.

If we were to rely on a diagnosis like ADHD or dyslexia in supporting and developing a child's learning capacity, it would be like staring at a blank map of the United States. We know we're in North America but have no idea how far north, south, east or west. In our experience, many kids with ADHD struggle with attention and working memory, but we've seen kids with an ADHD diagnosis score well on one or both of those tests. And it doesn't require an ADHD diagnosis to have weak attention or working memory skills. The bottom line is, figuring out how each child learns is absolutely critical. When we understand that, we can support and develop their learning capacity.

Here's an analogy we have found helpful. Let's say you have to clean a room in your house. You can do it with the lights on or the lights off. When we have a clearer understanding of a child's cognitive profile, it's like turning the lights on in a darkened room so that we can see the areas that need to be cleaned and make sure we're addressing those areas.

To use the map analogy, it's like having a GPS system. We can see where we are. We can pinpoint where we want to go. And we can plan the best route.

■ Practical and Insightful Assessment of Cognitive Skills

"The results of the Mindprint assessment were quite impressive. Our nine-year-old has been having some difficulties with math, specifically, a subject that had not previously been an issue. When her profile revealed a relative weakness in processing speed, some of the academic problems made more sense. The good news is that processing speed issues can be addressed. We had presumed that the issue had been working memory, and the assessment actually disproved this. In my professional life, I rely on data to make the most of my decisions. Conversely, I haven't had an opportunity to have such usable, precise and meaningful insight for my own child's educational development until now."

—Father of a nine-year-old girl

Using a nationally normed cognitive assessment allows us to do three very important things:

- First, it creates a baseline from which we can actually measure cognitive growth later.

- Second, it helps us personalize a child's cognitive training program. We've likened it to a GPS for learning. By determining where your child is now, the assessment naturally creates a roadmap for the training. For example, some children need to build specific skills before they can fully engage in and benefit from the exercises in BrainWare SAFARI. Or we may weave in work with other supplemental tools to extend and further challenge students who can benefit from it.

- And third, it allows us to provide specific, personalized recommendations for learning strategies that support weaker areas and take advantage of strengths. The education research literature has more "evidence-based strategies" than most people imagine. But not all strategies are suitable for every child. The key is to devise learning strategies targeted to each child's strengths and weaknesses and that work within whatever school or home-learning environment they operate in. Also, students need to cope with the dramatic changes COVID-19 created in instructional settings.

Ultimately, if your child gets behind in their learning, most schools don't have information on students' cognitive strengths and weaknesses and, therefore, have no tools to catch up. IEPs may help children progress some, but usually, every year, they fall further and further behind their peers.

The assessment process includes the national normed cognitive assessment referred to throughout this chapter and other components. Structured input from parents and sometimes teachers combine to give us a good picture of areas of strength and weakness and how they impact academics and life skills. The pieces of the assessment are all online and, in most cases, are completed by the family at home when they decide to go ahead.

The assessment results are shared with the family in an extensive report using parent-friendly language, and in an online meeting with one of our neuroeducators.

The process of sharing the assessment results is truly powerful. Parents will say, "That's my child!" or "Now I see why he/she struggles with XYZ!" There is usually a sense of relief. There is a reason for the struggles. And there is hope because cognitive skills can be developed and strengthened. Weak cognitive skills are not a life sentence. They are just a starting point.

"The reports are so spot on. The science is so accurate.
I am really thankful to God for providing us an
opportunity to use this for our daughter."

—Amita Devaraj, mother of Su (age eight)

Depending on the age and maturity of the child, we may also share the information on their cognitive profile with them. We use a report and conversation designed specifically for them. Children tend to be very aware of their struggles but have no idea why some things are so hard. Imbalances in the strength of different skills can make learning experiences very unpredictable for a child and, therefore, stressful. Because they don't know what's going to be hard and why, they tend to express feelings like, "I'm just stupid."

What we are able to show them and assure them is that they are not "stupid." They have cognitive strengths and weaknesses, just like every human being on the face of the earth. We explain their strengths (what we refer to as their "learning superpowers" when talking to them) and how they can use them. We discuss their weaker areas and explain how those can be strengthened through the program they will be going through. And we give them one or two things that they can do immediately to make learning more effective and less effortful.

We mentioned earlier that most assessments and discussions of a child's performance in school, especially in the context of an IEP, focus on weaknesses. Understanding a child's strengths and empowering them to take advantage of those strengths is perhaps even more important. When we explain their cognitive strengths and refer to them as learning superpowers, we help them understand how they can draw on their strengths in any learning situation. "Your superpower," we tell them, "is like the superhero cape in your closet. Whenever you find a learning situation difficult, you can put on that cape (use that power) to help you be successful."

Children find it empowering and, sometimes, surprising, to learn that they have strengths they can use and to be provided with personalized learning strategies (specific tools) that can help them.

Parents are often curious about what a personalized learning strategy might look like. Here are a couple of examples.

For most of us, our verbal memory (memory for language-based information that we read or hear) is stronger or weaker than our visual memory (memory for visual information such as images, charts, graphs, etc.).

Let's say that you are a student with stronger verbal memory. And your teacher assigns you a list of vocabulary words to learn. She asks you to write the word, write the definition of the word and write the word in a sentence. These activities, engaging with the new words using language, make a lot of sense.

Now, say that you are a student with stronger visual memory. That same assignment will be a very laborious and inefficient way for you to learn those vocabulary words. You can probably think of a better way – using pictures. As an aside, teachers would do well to try to help their students understand if they have uneven memory skills and support them in using memorization techniques that fit with how their brains work.

Here's another example. One child we worked with was very resistant to writing. He couldn't seem to put more than a sentence or a few words on paper. He couldn't think of what to say. He couldn't sequence his thoughts. He often couldn't even get started. Liam's cognitive assessment showed that his verbal reasoning skills – the ability to solve language-based problems and express something in words – were quite low. But his visual-spatial reasoning and visual memory were quite strong.

We suggested that Liam use a mind map to think about his topic before starting to write instead of using a traditional outline. A mind map is a way of creating visual representations of a topic and the relationships among ideas (sometimes also called a semantic map or an idea map). It allows the student to see (literally) how the elements of the topic and ideas relate to each other. Liam's mother used this technique the next time he had a writing assignment. She emailed us excitedly to say that he had written five coherent sentences without a battle. It will take Liam more practice with these techniques to get to the point where he can write five paragraphs or five pages rather than five sentences, but now he has a tool to help his amazing brain take what it understands and use it as the basis for other ways of expressing it.

When we help parents and kids understand their strengths and connect them to practical strategies, we can transform learning experiences. We can set expectations that are higher because we give them the tools to reach higher.

"I actually went through the program myself, twice, before I signed my children up. I saw changes in my ability to retain information and stay focused. I had experienced problems with focusing and retaining things in my memory – my kids get these things from me – I had to read pages more than once, and sometimes I would lose track and have to reread what I just read to understand it. Once I saw that I was able to retain information, read a page once and understand, it was like, okay, this is life-changing. I need to go talk to my kids and get them involved in the program.

"Joshua had been diagnosed with dyslexia as well as ADHD, and so I thought that the program would be beneficial to him to be able to focus and concentrate. He did not believe in himself as much as he should have. He did not believe that he could actually compete with the other kids. I can tell you that he has been able to remain focused and attentive in class this year, and that was difficult for him before. The program gave him a level of self-confidence that he did not have before.

"Rachel's issue was a bit different. She kind of lacked motivation. She would not challenge herself with difficult tasks. She would always do the things that she thought she could achieve very easily, and she would avoid anything that she thought was too difficult. Rachel benefited from the program because now she's more willing to try even if she struggles a little bit. One of the main problems we had with Rachel was that she struggled as a reader. She couldn't even force herself to finish a page before she would get tired or frustrated and just decide to stop. About halfway through the program, she was actually able to start reading and became a more confident reader. Now she finishes books in one day as opposed to reading one page of a book and stopping. She would read a whole book in one day and then ask for the next book in the series, which was totally shocking to me.

"If you've experienced issues with your child either not being able to focus, not being able to keep up with the other kids in class, or even having issues with self-confidence and in their ability in their academic performance, then they should definitely take a look at the BrainWare SAFARI program. I don't think it is just for kids with dyslexia or ADHD. I think it can be beneficial for all kids because it helps with the basic underlying structure and enables the child to learn and build on top of these because if you can't recognize symbols, if you can't retain information in your head for long periods of time, there's no way you could be a great reader, there's no way you can do challenging mathematical operations. Once you focus on those underlying foundational topics and build on those, then you can go on to more challenging topics and become a more proficient reader and a better mathematician."

—Tony Lockhart, father of Joshua (age twelve) and Rachel (age eight)

CHAPTER FOUR

Step #3 Build the Cognitive Foundation for Learning

"BrainWare SAFARI works on the skills that can benefit children for their lifetime. Other skills they may forget, but this is different. It's like Chinese traditional medicine; it cures from the root."

—Dr. Puling Z, mother of Rachel (age seven)

◼ Cognitive Skills: The Foundation for Learning

The third step is to build the cognitive foundation for learning. We've referred to cognitive skills and cognitive training in the previous chapters. This chapter will dig in deeper. This is where you'll learn about the cognitive skills that form the foundation for learning. Just like a house needs a strong foundation, so does learning. And cognitive skills form the foundation for academic success and everything we do in life. In the first part of this chapter, we'll explain what cognitive skills are and how they relate to academics and behavior. In the second part, we'll review how they can be trained and the kind of impact that cognitive training can have.

Here is a chart that we have found helpful in framing our discussion of cognitive skills.

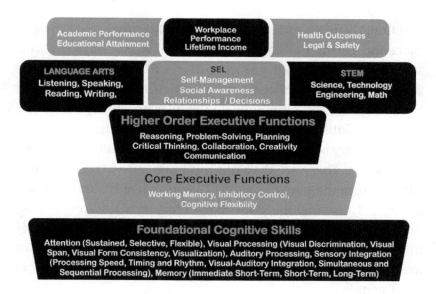

Figure 7. Cognitive skills are the foundation for learning.

Up at the top of this chart are the goals we have for our children. These include getting as far as they can and as far as they want to academically. The goals include getting a good job that supports them and their families and that they find satisfying. And they include being a healthy and contributing member of society.

Just below that, at the second tier in the chart, is where schools focus: on reading, math and the rest of the curriculum. And schools are starting to focus more these days on social and emotional learning. SEL (Social and Emotional Learning) refers to the mindsets and skills that we use to manage ourselves, relate to others, and make good decisions. You can think of SEL as dealing with EQ (Emotional Quotient, or emotional intelligence).

While people sometimes think that reading and writing, and math are the basics, there are even more basic skills.

Often, little attention is paid to the skills that need to be in place for learning to happen at the level where schools focus. We refer to these skills as cognitive skills and they are the foundation or the infrastructure for learning. A foundation, beams, wiring and plumbing are the infrastructure for a house. Cognitive skills are the infrastructure for learning.

At the very base of our model, you will see foundational cognitive skills. These are the skills our brains use to take in information from the outside world. That's what starts the learning process. These include skills like attention, visual processing, auditory processing and processing speed. You are probably already very tuned in to how important attention and focus are. But there are a whole bunch of other skills at this level that most people don't think about all the time.

If their foundational skills are working accurately and efficiently, your child isn't even aware of them. The start of the learning process is effortless. But if they can't sustain their attention or screen out distractions, or if other foundational skills are weak, the very beginning of the learning process can be a huge stumbling block.

Then, at the next level up in the chart, there is a special category of cognitive skills called executive functions. Executive functions are some of the biggest predictors of academic and life success, so they're really important. These are the skills we use to regulate our behavior, organize and keep track of our learning, and adapt to changing conditions. If someone has strong executive functions, we know they are far more likely to succeed in school and post-secondary education, to make more money, to have a happier marriage and be healthier as an adult. In fact, everything at the top of the chart can be predicted to a significant degree by the skills at the bottom of the chart.

And then, we have the level of higher-order executive

functions. If you've ever heard someone talk about 21st-century skills, this is a good starting list. These are also skills that most employers put at the top of their hiring criteria – oftentimes higher than technical knowledge or subject-matter expertise. We'll explain that more later in this chapter.

"To educate students in the Information Age instead of the Industrial Age, we need Information Age tools and materials that support Information Age thinking. BrainWare SAFARI is on the cutting edge of preparing students to be Information Age thinkers using exercises that develop their ability to recognize patterns, solve problems, and think more effectively."

—Ron Kraft, School District Superintendent, MI

Cognitive Skills

Let's dig into some specific cognitive skills, starting with some categories of foundational cognitive skills.

"When you say to kids, 'Pay attention!' you've got a lot of kids who try but don't know how to do it. They don't have the basic skills to pay attention."

—Pat Wolfe

ATTENTION SKILLS

Typically, when you or your child's teacher talk about "attention," you are referring to your child's ability to stay on task and to focus on the task at hand. This is sustained attention. Another attention skill is the ability to screen out distractions (selective attention). Selective attention is often more of a problem for individuals with ADHD than sustained attention. They can be easily distracted and taken off track. The ability to alternate our focus between two things (cooking dinner and watching what the kids are doing) is referred to as divided attention. Then there is flexible attention, how efficiently we shift our focus from one task to another. And finally, for sustained or selective attention, we can be stronger or weaker at attending to visual or auditory information.

So here is a list of six attention skills that play an important role in determining whether the information we need is even getting into our brains to start the learning process.

1. **Visual Sustained Attention** – The ability to stay on task for a sustained period, dealing with visual information (sight).

2. **Auditory Sustained Attention** – The ability to stay on task for a sustained period, dealing with auditory information (sound).

3. **Visual Selective Attention** – The ability to pay attention to one input while not being distracted by other inputs, dealing with visual information (sight).

4. **Auditory Selective Attention** – The ability to pay attention to one input while not being distracted by other inputs, dealing with auditory information (sound).

5. **Divided Attention** – The ability to pay attention to two activities at the same time, like taking notes while listening to the teacher.

6. **Flexible Attention** – The ability to shift focus from one task to another quickly and efficiently, when necessary.

Today, we often hear a colleague say (or maybe we say this ourselves), "That's my ADHD." The pace and demands of today's world make it harder than ever to concentrate and stay focused on one thing. In most cases, it probably doesn't rise to an ADHD diagnosis. However, it's important to understand that many kids and many adults still struggle with aspects of attention nonetheless. If you think of yourself, your spouse, friends and your children, you can probably name someone (or more than one!) who has a weakness in one of the six attention skills listed above.

VISUAL PROCESSING SKILLS

Visual processing skills help us make sense of what is seen in the world around us. When most people think of visual processing, the first thing that comes to mind may be the measure of eyesight we have heard in the doctor's office. When you are told that your child's eyesight is 20/20, all that means is that your child can see what an average person can see on an eye chart at a distance of 20 feet. It is a measure of acuity. It is not a measure of overall visual processing.

Another aspect of visual processing is the various vision mechanics that affect the way visual information is received in the brain. These include how well the eyes focus, accommodate (adjust to different distances), how efficient the eye movements are, convergence (how the eyes turn inward as an object gets closer), and how the eyes work together to create binocular vision (depth perception). All of these processes will determine how good the visual information is that gets into your child's brain. After the visual information is received in the brain, then the visual processing areas in the brain have to make sense of that incoming information.

Don't our brains automatically make sense of what we see? In a sense, yes. Our brains are meaning-making machines and we recognize what we see by comparing the visual input to what we have stored in our brains from our previous experience. But think about optical illusions you may be familiar with. Optical illusions are designed to be ambiguous and different people may see different things, But let's think about a visual perception task that isn't designed to be tricky.

Let's say you're looking for your keys. You glance around the room and you see them peeking out from underneath a piece of paper on the counter. You still recognize them as your keys, even though they are partially hidden from you. You see them as your keys even though your brain isn't actually taking in a complete set of visual data about them. You can also recognize your keys when you see them from the top, the bottom, the side, and so on. This is called visual form consistency – perceiving visual information about an object consistently even though it is not presented in its most obvious manner. We can all miss things from time to time, but if you have a child who consistently cannot find his backpack when it is in a pile of his belongings, visual form consistency could be an issue.

Visual span is another cognitive skill that is important in reading, in sports and in driving. Visual span is the ability to take in a bunch of information at a glance. You probably know the term "peripheral vision." That is what you are aware of at the outer edges of your field of vision. This is a familiar term because we know it helps us drive (seeing cars that are about to pass us). But many people don't know the terms for other parts of our field of vision. Center vision is the term for the words that we are focused on when we read, for example. Visual span relates to our ability to use our center vision and our peripheral vision together. When we can, we can see more information – groups of words or even more – in a single glance.

Visualization is another extremely important visual processing skill. Close your eyes and imagine a pink elephant with a purple trunk and dark blue tusks ... wearing a tutu. Our brains can see things that don't exist. And our brains can "see things" that aren't in front of us right now. Think back to your bedroom when you were thirteen. What color were the walls? You can see them, right? Visualization will turn out to be a very important part of reading comprehension and geometry, as well as many other really useful things.

Descriptions of some other visual processing skills (as well as other cognitive processes) can be found in Appendix 1.

AUDITORY PROCESSING SKILLS

Auditory processing skills help us make sense of what we hear in the world around us, just as visual processing skills help us make sense of what we see in the world around us. If a child's hearing is normal, they can still have difficulty with listening, reading comprehension, and miscommunication that causes trouble with parents, teachers, family and friends. For example, your child may misunderstand directions, become frustrated when trying to follow oral instructions, and seem like they are ignoring you.

One important auditory processing skill is auditory discrimination. This is the ability to distinguish between two similar sounds. Even if your hearing is generally good, you may still have difficulty deciding whether someone said, "Please pass me the gun," or "Please pass me the gum," in a noisy room. Most of us can figure out which one was meant, but some people don't actually hear the difference.

Auditory sequential processing refers to the way our brains keep information in the order we receive it. It seems obvious that our brains would do this, but sometimes it isn't so easy. Some children confuse the order of numbers (was that 75 or 57?) or can't keep track of the order of tasks even when they can remember them.

"My daughter has Sensory Processing Disorder; her vision and auditory system are impacted by this. BrainWare SAFARI does a great job targeting the skills she needs improvement on. We've found some of the games are similar to exercises her vision therapist was having her do, though BrainWare does it in a way that's more fun. As a parent, I enjoy watching her play the games and find them challenging for myself."

—J. Detweiler, father of an eight-year-old girl

SENSORY INTEGRATION SKILLS

Talk about brainpower! Sensory integration is the processing in the brain that takes the information received from our five senses, organizes it, and responds appropriately. It puts the visual and auditory information we are taking in into a coherent whole and lets us act on it.

Often, students have strengths and weaknesses that create an imbalance in their sensory integration abilities. However, even very successful students find that by improving the sensory integration functions of their brains, they can achieve better results.

Have you ever had the experience of watching a movie when the sound is slightly behind or slightly ahead of the visual? It is hard to combine the inputs into a coherent whole. Sensory integration enables our brains to create a whole out of disparate parts.

PROCESSING SPEED

We have all probably had the experience of not being able to respond to a remark or something that somebody does or says as quickly as we would like. It's very common in a stressful situation, as when someone insults or unfairly criticizes you. You may have come up with the perfect comeback but not until the next day. That's because cognition is slowed down in states of stress. For some students, responding slowly is an everyday, all-the-time problem.

Processing speed is the speed at which our brains work, the pace at which we can take in information and do something. Processing speed varies. Some brains are just faster than others. But it is essential to understand that processing speed is not the same as intelligence. Nor does having a slower processing speed mean that someone is less intelligent.

We have to be really careful because we often hear comments like, *"Oh well, that person is just slow."* Or, *"She's just slower than everybody else."* And you might very well assume that they're not very smart, but as we'll see, slow processing speed often comes with high intelligence. We also have to recognize that our brains may process different kinds of inputs at different rates.

This can be confusing because processing speed can be inconsistent even within the same person. A child may have high processing speed for visual information when they play a video game, for example, but have a lot of trouble with auditory information when they hear a parent or a teacher give them a set of instructions. Many parents have been in that situation. *"I don't understand why he can't respond quickly! Why is he so responsive when he's playing a video game, but not when it comes to other things?"*

Slow processing speed can look like having difficulty making even a simple decision. *"What do you want for breakfast?" "What shirt do you want to wear?"* When a child is asked that kind of question and has difficulty processing it and responding, they may take a long time to respond, or they may just blurt something out and immediately feel that it's not really what they wanted. It can be very stressful and confusing because they know you're waiting for their response, but they haven't fully processed it.

"Seven years ago, when Justin started using BrainWare, he was confused by it at first. Once he was able to understand it, he enjoyed it, and it led to much better hand-eye coordination as well as working faster and with enhanced comprehension. I believe the exposure to BrainWare assisted him in coming off his 504 status, because he was able to finish tests in the standard classroom time. He has also become more social."

—Scott W., father of Justin (age fifteen)

Let's take a concrete example of what slower processing speed might look like. If you ask a child to pick up their LEGOs and get started on homework and they don't get immediately at the task of picking up those LEGOs, it may be because it takes them a while to process what it actually means. What does mom actually mean when she says pick them up? Pick them up and do what with them? All of them or just the ones in the path to the kitchen? By the time they process what picking up LEGOs means, the fact that mom also said something about homework may no longer be something that their brain is holding onto for them.

Kids with slow processing speed often dread tests or anything that sounds like a speed drill. So, a math fluency test, a reading speed test or a quick drill on the basketball court may all result in anxiety or even a meltdown. Think of something that you know how to do well but that you don't do very quickly, so you may do it slowly, but the end result is a very good piece of work. For Betsy, that's knitting. If she felt she was being judged by how long it takes her to knit rather than the quality of the baby blanket she's currently working on, she might do what many kids will do – avoid it.

Slow processing speed can also look like awkwardness in social situations. If it takes a while to process what someone is saying, it can look like not paying attention, like you don't care, or like you don't think what they're saying is important. And it may take longer to pick up on social cues, like a delayed response when the teacher asks the class to be quiet.

Just about every parent of a child with slow processing speed is familiar with what can become the agony of dealing with homework. A reasonable length assignment may take far longer than it should be or than the teacher ever intended. Sometimes it's just even about getting started on that homework.

We tend to be more aware of issues with slow processing speed, but processing speed that is very fast can also cause difficulties. Parents of children with faster processing may see issues with "careless errors" – simply working too fast to carefully consider what is being worked on – and lower accuracy.

"Our daughter had high reasoning ability but relatively low processing speed. This caused anxiety, and she was not able to shine, to show how beautiful her brain was and how well it worked. Our daughter was very enthusiastic about the BrainWare program, especially the video gaming aspect. We started seeing progress in the first two weeks. Her anxiety level was much lower, and she was willing to take on new things. We had a lovely BrainWare coach named Annette who helped our daughter and had a very positive effect on me, showing me how to work with my daughter. Towards the end of it, Su's anxiety practically vanished. I would describe the BrainWare program as life-changing because of a number of positive changes I have seen in my daughter as well as myself."

—Amita Devarj and Mahesh Ganesh, parents of Su (age eight)

MEMORY SKILLS

When we use the term memory, we tend to think simplistically about learning something (committing it to memory) and then being able to remember it later. We often talk about memory storage as if memory were a separate place in the brain, like a storage vault. Sometimes that's a helpful analogy, but memory doesn't actually work that way.

Remember how we defined learning earlier in the book? We said that learning is the process of creating and strengthening connections among neurons into neural networks in our brains. Memory, then, is the process of reactivating the networks of neurons that were earlier created and strengthened. The stronger the connections among those neurons, the easier it is to reactivate the memory later. Or, as neuroscientists put it, "neurons that fire together, wire together." The firing of a neuron refers to it being activated and sending messages to other neurons in that network.

It is useful (although overly simplified) to divide memory into short-term and long-term memory. Short-term memory is our ability to hold onto information for a short time (say, ten minutes or a few hours). If we asked you to remember what you had for breakfast, that information is in short-term memory. If we asked you to remember what you had for breakfast three days ago, you might have a lot more difficulty recalling that information (unless you have the same thing for breakfast every day). That's because our brains don't remember unimportant information. The network that stored that breakfast memory may be reused or modified in the course of other things that happen during the day.

Information that we are holding in short-term memory has to go through additional processing to be stored in long-term memory. There's a tiny structure in our brains called the hippocampus that is responsible for this. So, if memory isn't processed in that way, it doesn't get stored as long-term memory and can't be retrieved.

Memory skills are, of course, exceedingly important since remembering is inherent in learning. We can't really be said to have learned something if we can't retrieve the information.

Long-term memory and short-term memory can also be divided into distinct cognitive processes. Short-term memory, for example, includes sensory memory, which refers to our brain's ability to hold onto the information coming in through our senses for a few thousandths of a second. Another type of short-term memory allows us to hold onto information for a bit longer, say, to remember back to know who came into the classroom ten minutes ago. Long-term memory can be divided into different types as well. And both types of memory skills can be different for different types of information. Most of us have different levels of skill for verbal memory (memory for language-based information we hear or read) and for visual memory (memory for images, charts, diagrams, etc.)

Understanding whether your child has stronger visual or verbal long-term memory can be very helpful in providing them with specific strategies to help them memorize different types of information more efficiently and with less effort.

Here we need to make a distinction between cognitive processes and the concept of "learning styles." The value of learning styles has been thoroughly debunked, although many people (including most educators, based on surveys) still believe that adapting instructions to a person's preferred learning style is important. Research has shown that trying to cater to an individual's preference (visual, auditory, kinesthetic) and presenting information in that one way is ineffective (and generally counterproductive) When we talk about learning strategies based on an individual's cognitive strengths and weaknesses, we are not talking about learning styles. We are talking about providing each child with strategies to help them use their cognitive strengths to better understand and learn whatever information they encounter.

EXECUTIVE FUNCTIONS

Executive Functions are the directive capacities of our brains – how we manage information, plan and decide, act or stop ourselves from acting, and adapt to unexpected situations.

While individual cognitive skills can be stronger or weaker, it is the elegance of the choreography, the way all these capacities integrate, flow and work together that makes up our overall intelligence.

Executive Functions play a vital role in the choreography. Sometimes people use the analogy of the orchestra conductor where the brain's processes are the instruments in the orchestra, all coordinated by the conductor. Another analogy is an air traffic control center.

Executive Functions are how our brains organize all our mental processes toward goal-directed, purposeful behavior. Many parents and teachers think of Executive Functions as self-regulation, which is an important aspect of these types of cognitive skills. Still, there is a lot more to it than that. And like all cognitive skills, Executive Functions play a role in learning and just about everything we do in our lives.

There are three core Executive Functions:

1. Working Memory is our conscious processing. Working memory allows you to hold onto information while you think about it or act on it. When someone gives you directions, or says their name when you are introduced,

or when you do mental math, that is happening in working memory. One important aspect of working memory is that it is limited. While our brains can hold a seemingly limitless amount of information in long-term memory, we can only keep a fairly small amount active in conscious thought.

2. Inhibitory Control is the ability to suppress a thought or idea and to refrain from doing something we otherwise would do. When you stop yourself from speaking in order not to interrupt someone, or decide to stay in and study for a test rather than going to a party, that is inhibitory control.

3. Cognitive Flexibility is the ability to change our mindset and adapt when things change around us or shift between mental processes. It also helps us see things from different perspectives. The constant changes we have all experienced during the COVID-19 pandemic have put increased demands on cognitive flexibility for all of us.

WHAT READING AND BIRTHDAY CAKES HAVE IN COMMON

It is important to understand that the cognitive skills we have been talking about apply to everything we do in life, whether it is reading, math, making toast for breakfast or planning a complex project. That seems pretty obvious when we are talking about attention or visual processing. Still, it isn't always intuitive when it comes to Executive Functions. Frequently, we hear people use the term Executive Functions as if they only apply to social and emotional learning – self-regulation, seeing different points of view, and the like. One of the most important things to understand about Executive Functions is that they are essential in reading, math, and other academic subjects. They are also vital in building social and emotional competence. In other words, Working Memory is the same mental process whether we are using it to comprehend what we are reading, to solve a complex math problem, or to consider what someone else is saying and what might be causing them to say it.

Let's take one most parents understand intuitively, inhibitory control. The lack of inhibitory control is what we often refer to as impulsivity. Weaknesses in inhibitory control show up in reading ⊠ when a student "blurts out" or "guesses" words ⊠ and, of course, in social situations, such as when a child punches someone when they're mad or blows out the candles on someone else's birthday cake. In other words, what birthday cakes and reading have in common is a need for inhibitory control.

Inhibitory control is the same process in our brains, for academics and for social behavior, just in a different context. We tend to think of academic skills and behavior differently, but the fact is, the same cognitive processes serve as the foundation for both.

"We are a STEM [Science, Technology, Engineering and Math] building, so problem-based and project-based learning are a big push for us. What we found is we had a lot of kids who came to school, they worked hard, they did the work, and for some reason, the connections just weren't being made to higher-order thinking. They might even be an A and B student because they could 'play school,' but what we found was that they struggled with some of the core executive functions of working memory and cognitive flexibility. If you ask them a lower-level thinking question like the capital of a country, they could do it, but the moment you gave them a project, maybe something with very little instruction and only a rubric to go on, they fell apart.

"Another area that is really interesting to me is inhibitory control. We found that kiddos who struggled behaviorally were actually lacking in those core functions, and it wasn't a necessary choice that they made. It was something that they just couldn't do; they've got to just blurt it out.

"We did a cognitive test to start and found that 92 percent of my kids were at risk for attention and/or working memory. We knew right then and there that this was going to be a group of kiddos that would totally benefit from increased cognitive functioning. BrainWare SAFARI gave them an opportunity in a very non-threatening way to practice thinking, to practice molding things in their mind and build their confidence. BrainWare has taken something from the clinical setting and brought it to kids and brought it to schools, and for that, I am eternally grateful.

"It's no longer a pilot for us. It is how we do things, and it's part of our intervention structure. The kids who took BrainWare and did it the right way absolutely every single one of them got 10-plus, scale-score point gains, and 55 percent were on track to gain two years' growth during this year. Our kids are showing an appreciable difference in their ability to learn, their ability to think and their ability to progress at more than a grade level per year. The only way to meet the demands of what these kids are coming to us with, especially in a middle school where they're coming to us 80 percent not at grade level, is for them to show two years growth. That is our absolute goal that every single one of our kids is making progress not only towards a year but making progress towards grade-level proficiency. And the only way we have found is for our kiddos to be in both BrainWare and their reading intervention, as well as their Gen Ed Math, their Gen Ed English, their science and their social studies the way they're supposed to be getting grade-level standards. This isn't about dumbing it down. This isn't about anything other than meeting kids where they're at with their cognitive ability, their reading ability, as well as their confidence.

"The reason why they're struggling with school and learning and thinking and the reason why they have a defeatist attitude is because they just can't. This has given them absolutely the tools to do school and so with that renewed ability and that renewed confidence we're seeing just absolutely astronomical growth."

—Tom Hughes, principal, Maple Crest Middle School, Kokomo, IN

PARENT KEY 12

Cognitive Skills are the same mental processes whether we are using them for reading or math or having a conversation.

The chart below provides a quick overview of the role Executive Functions play in academics and social and emotional learning. Following the chart, we'll provide both academic and social (behavioral) examples of each.

WORKING MEMORY

WHAT IT IS: The ability to hold information in our mind while we think about it.

ACADEMIC IMPACT: Holding multiple aspects of a problem in mind and keeping track of where we are in a multi-step solution.

SOCIAL/EMOTIONAL EXAMPLE: Holding someone else's point of view in mind, comparing and contrasting it to other points of view, considering alternative ways to respond.

INHIBITORY CONTROL

WHAT IT IS: The ability to suppress a thought or idea, to refrain from doing something we otherwise would.

ACADEMIC IMPACT: Not leaping to the first possible solution but questioning assumptions and considering other alternatives.

SOCIAL/EMOTIONAL EXAMPLE: Not blowing out the candles on someone else's birthday cake. Not blurting out "That's stupid," when you disagree. Also, deferring gratification (longer term).

COGNITIVE FLEXIBILITY

WHAT IT IS: The ability to change our mindset when the rules of the world around us change.

ACADEMIC IMPACT: When our original approach to a problem doesn't work, finding other approaches. Looking at problems from different points of view and being able to change direction on the basis of new information.

SOCIAL/EMOTIONAL EXAMPLE: Looking at personal experiences from different points of view and being able to change direction on the basis of new information.

Figure 8. Executive Functions academic and social/emotional impact.

WORKING MEMORY EXAMPLES

In reading, working memory is our conscious processing of what we are reading. It is how we hold onto the beginning of the sentence or paragraph until we get to the end. It is how we compare what we are reading to what we already know, which is how we give something meaning. Working memory is vital for comprehension. Limited working memory capacity is a factor in many students who can read fluently but seem to have little idea afterward what they read.

In math, working memory is involved in everything from copying a problem from the board or the math book to one's paper, to counting and keeping track of which items have been counted and which haven't, to tracking the steps of a complex algebra problem.

Working memory helps us follow the train of a conversation in social situations – who has said what – and the general flow. It is also where we hold onto a set of instructions that someone gives us while carrying them out. Poor working memory capacity can look like a lack of attention or caring. If a child can't remember what they were supposed to do, it can look like they don't care, weren't paying attention, or are just plain lazy or even obstinate.

INHIBITORY CONTROL EXAMPLES

In reading, inhibitory control is involved in selecting among word candidates in decoding (identifying words from their written form). "Blurting" words out is due more to a lack of inhibitory control than of mere guessing, according to the research.

In math, inhibitory control helps us wait to multiply numbers until we've added the ones in parentheses or treat a negative number differently from a positive one. It is critical for math that is non-intuitive, where we need to suppress what we think makes sense to do the mathematical analysis or apply the principle that will help us get the appropriate solution.

In social and emotional learning, inhibitory control is the peak of self-regulation. The scenario we described above (blowing out the candles on someone else's birthday cake) is one example. You can probably think of myriad examples yourself, from not punching someone in the face when you get mad at them to waiting to cross the street until the light turns green. It is also important in the longer term when we postpone immediate self-gratification for a greater goal. (Put down that doughnut!)

COGNITIVE FLEXIBILITY EXAMPLES

In reading, cognitive flexibility enables us to switch smoothly between the brain systems we use to sound out words and recognize sight words. It allows us to switch our attention between word meaning, grammar, syntax, and overall meaning and relate to different characters within a narrative.

In math, cognitive flexibility helps us adjust when an initial approach to solving a problem doesn't work or to choose among various possible ways to solve a problem, depending on whether we are emphasizing speed or accuracy. It is also important when the question to be solved is not intuitive.

In social behavior, cognitive flexibility helps us stop an activity we are involved in and transition to another activity. It allows us to change our minds when we learn new information (e.g., the world is round, not flat), make relevant cognitive adjustments, and recognize the implications. It is what helps us recognize our mental models and consider alternative explanations for what we see happening in the world.

HIGHER-ORDER EXECUTIVE FUNCTIONS

Higher-order executive functions are the complex thinking processes that we use to interpret and understand how things work in the world around us. Logic helps us ascribe cause and effect to events. The train was late; therefore, I missed the appointment. It snowed heavily overnight, so the fresh footprints in the snow must be those of the newspaper delivery person. Of course, if the newspaper hasn't been delivered, we may need to think of other explanations (cognitive flexibility).

Reasoning skills are how we form ideas and concepts and derive meaning from non-literal information. In the context of learning, it is helpful to distinguish among three types of complex reasoning skills; verbal reasoning, abstract reasoning, and spatial reasoning.

Verbal reasoning is the ability to understand the nuances of language-based information. Drawing inferences, interpreting figurative language (a sunny smile, a stormy expression), and using analogies and metaphors (being up the creek in a canoe without a paddle).

Abstract reasoning is the ability to see patterns (similarities and differences) and group information based on traits. Abstract reasoning is also referred to as nonverbal reasoning, so an example makes more sense than trying to describe it.

Which image belongs in the box with the ??

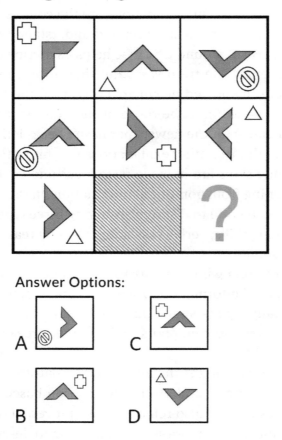

Figure 9. Abstract reasoning puzzle. The correct answer is at the end of the chapter.

Spatial Reasoning involves our ability to rotate shapes, use 3-D models and understand how shapes relate to each other. Parallel parking involves spatial reasoning, as do any of the "assembly required" presents you've ever spent hours trying to put together, or figuring out how to get all the luggage into the trunk of the car. Here's an example of a puzzle that requires spatial reasoning.

Shape Rotation Puzzle (spatial reasoning)

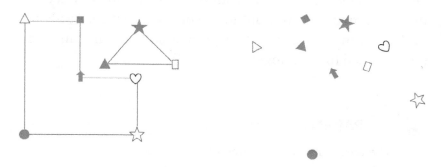

Figure 10. Can you draw lines between the small shapes on the right so that they create the two larger shapes on the left? The shapes are the same but rotated in space. Hint: The shapes may overlap. The correct answer is at the end of the chapter.

"I am very pleased with BrainWare Learning Company! They have amazing founders who truly want to help our children succeed in whichever education system our kids participate. I have two kids who are benefiting from their program. The coach working with them is very kind and patient and expects hard work, focus, accountability, and responsibility. She does an amazing job with my children. After working with them for four weeks, I have seen dramatic improvements in their focus, desire to learn, self-start homework and schoolwork, and problem-solving. I have seen their confidence in their ability to research, learn, and apply, grow!!"

—Renae T., mother of Michael (age fourteen) and Allison (age seventeen)

Now that we've explored some important cognitive skills and how they play a role in reading, math and social and emotional competence, we want to flip our perspective. Academic skills depend not just on one cognitive skill but on many, and they all need to work together.

PARENT KEY 13

The basics are not the three R's – reading, writing and 'rithmetic, or the other subjects that are usually taught in school. Cognitive skills are the real basics for learning.

Cognitive Skills and Reading

"Basics" of Reading

Decoding   Fluency   Comprehension

When educators talk about the basics of reading, they usually are thinking about three skills.

1. **Decoding** – Sounding out words and recognizing sight words.

2. **Fluency** – Building up the ability to flow as they read (reading more quickly and with expression).

3. **Comprehension** – Understanding what the text means, which is the ultimate purpose of reading.

If you can't comprehend, you can't read. These three skills are essential, but they are not the most basic.

Recently, we've begun to hear this kind of statement from parents, "He can decode words, and his fluency is good, but he struggles with comprehension the most. Without comprehension, he can't go that far."

What's happened today is that the education system treats reading as if it were three independent processes. Then they measure them separately. They determine whether a child can read a word out loud correctly. Then they measure the speed with which they read correctly. And then they measure whether they understood what they read. As if these were independent processes. That is why you can hear a teacher say that a child is making progress in reading, or even "reading at grade level," even though they don't understand what they read. They may be decoding grade-level words. They may be reading at the same pace as their grade-level peers. So, on two of three measures, they're at grade level. But the reality is, if your child can't comprehend, they really can't read. That's the bottom line.

And parents tell us, "I don't want my child to continue feeling they know how to read when they don't comprehend. I told the teacher we have to work on comprehension, but it isn't making any difference even after two years!"

We need to dig down to the real basics to understand what's really going on when a child learns to read.

To get more specific, let's start with decoding. There is no decoding part of the brain. To decode or sound out words, our brains have to organize a bunch of processes that all need to work together. So, for example, imagine your child loses focus partway through sounding out a word. Then, they have to start all over again. That's a problem. If they are slow in processing information, it's hard to build up fluency to read at the rate needed for expression and comprehension. And comprehension depends a lot on working memory and visualization, among other skills. The diagram below shows some of the most important cognitive skills that are the true basics of reading.

Cognitive Processes Associated with Reading

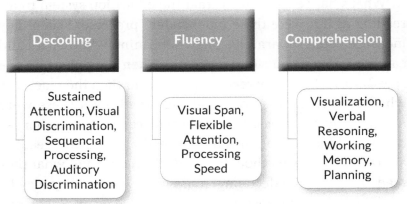

Figure 11. The "basics" of reading rely on multiple underlying cognitive skills.

◾ Cognitive Skills and Math

'Basics" of Math

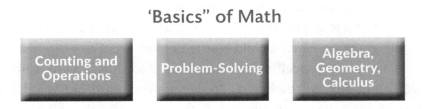

Then we get to math. Similar principles apply here. When it comes to determining whether a child is performing grade-level math, teachers usually refer to the topics that are commonly taught at a particular grade level. It starts with counting and basic arithmetic operations – addition, subtraction, multiplication, division, telling time, money, decimals, ratios, etc., all the way up to geometry and calculus (and beyond). Math is often treated as a bunch of independent processes (sets of steps) rather than concepts and meaning. And math instruction often ignores the even more basic underlying cognitive processes our brains need to learn to do math.

Cognitive Processes Associated with Math

Counting and Operations	Problem-Solving	Algebra, Geometry, Calculus
Sequential Processing, Selective Attention, Working Memory, Long-Term Memory	Planning, Sequential Processing, Working Memory, Verbal Reasoning, Cognitive Flexibility	Spatial Perception, Visualization, Directionality, Abstract Reasoning

Figure 12. The basics of math rely on multiple underlying cognitive skills.

Once again, the cognitive skills needed for math are where the real story is. Let's take some examples again, starting with the simple process of counting. Let's say we need to count the number of people in a room (perhaps to see if the room's capacity is being exceeded). We have to keep track of which people we've counted and which we haven't. That process happens in working memory. Even the seemingly simplest math task requires working memory!

The same is true for problem-solving. Sequential processing helps us keep the steps we need to go through in the right order. Working memory helps us track where we are and keep multiple aspects of a complex problem in mind. Logic and reasoning are needed to reason through relationships, and cognitive flexibility is what we call on if we need to shift directions and try a different tack.

Visual-spatial skills come into play with math topics like algebra, geometry and calculus. Let's say we have to interpret information from a graph. We're going to use our visualization and directionality skills to derive meaning from the information. But we don't have to be engaged with advanced math to need visual-spatial skills. Let's go back to our example of counting people in a room. Let's say, as we might during some of the restrictions in the COVID era, that we need to assess whether people are staying about six feet apart. Spatial perception will help or hinder us from doing that.

If you've noticed that many of the cognitive skills we've identified as the true basics of learning are the same for reading and math, pat yourself on the back. We have just one brain for reading and math. And of course, we also use these skills for everything else we do because it isn't all just about academics. We use these same skills in everyday life and in everything we do and think about. Cognitive skills are the same mental processes, whatever context they arise in.

Cognitive Strengths and Weaknesses

We all have cognitive strengths and weaknesses. As competent adults, we have learned to work around our weaknesses, but we may become very aware of them when confronted with certain kinds of tasks or see someone else do something with ease that would take us far more effort. But for kids who struggle with learning, weaker cognitive areas can be real stumbling blocks. Those stumbling blocks are like black-out curtains keeping a child's strengths from shining.

Maybe a kid with weaker cognitive skills will figure out how to compensate or work around and find success in spite of the stumbling blocks. But if they don't, two things are likely to happen. First, they'll lose self-esteem, become anxious, and just give up. Or, even if they keep at it, they will put such enormous effort into trying to do what they're asked that they become exhausted.

If you know what the stumbling blocks are, you have a real opportunity to do something about it. Remember that cognitive skills account for 50 percent of the variability in academic performance and that 50 percent rests within your power as a parent to change for your child.

In the last chapter, we talked about how we can identify a students' cognitive strengths and weaker areas. Now we can consider what to do to address them.

Urey Middle School in the John Glenn School District in Walkerton, Indiana, provides a model for how assessing cognitive skills and then strengthening them can lead to academic performance gains for students. In the 2021-2022 school year, under the leadership of the school's principal, Gregg Goewert, all of the seventh-grade students took an initial cognitive assessment. Teachers and students were educated on how to use the information to improve students' study skills. Then two cohorts of students worked in BrainWare SAFARI for a semester.

"We are very proud of the 20 percent average gain in executive function/cognitive skills (across the continuum)," Gregg said. "It's the JG [John Glenn] way that kids and our community will work hard. We have seen the thirty-two kids do better academically with all of their grades, Clearsight [benchmark testing], and we are going to gather narrative data from the teaching staff/aides/parents on growth the adults working with these students have observed. We believe this program is indeed as marketed – a very scientific program to help grow executive function and cognitive skills."

Data collected at the end of school year showed that seventy-one percent of the 7th-grade students in the cognitive training program improved their Reading and or Math scores on the ILEARN state standardized assessment.

The Old Way vs. the New Way

What all of this discussion of cognitive skills means is that the traditional ways of helping struggling learners are inadequate. To explain, we'll talk about two different approaches – what we call the old way of helping struggling learners vs the new way.

THE OLD WAY

The old way is to bypass the cognitive processes that are weak to minimize the impact. What exactly does this mean? The old way has three main approaches – accommodations, modifications to the curriculum and compensatory strategies.

You and your child may very well have experienced accommodations. These are things like giving a child extra time to complete a task, helping them with notetaking, giving them verbal and written instructions, or having your child sit in a specific place in the classroom.

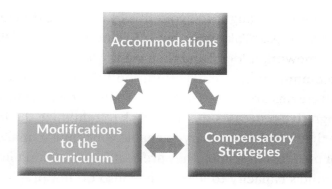

Figure 13. The old way strategies to address weak cognitive skills.

Modifications to the curriculum are another thing you may have experienced. These modifications could be a book written at a different grade level or books with pictures instead of a lot of text, fewer spelling words, or fewer math problems to do as homework. With these modifications, your child does not have to live up to the standards set for the typically progressing students. And in fact, a lot of this really is built around helping your child make some sort of progress, not necessarily the progress expected to reach grade level proficiency.

And lastly, the old way often involves compensatory strategies. And here's a concrete example. Let's take working memory again. If your child has an issue with working memory, which is very common, they may have difficulty with a set of instructions. Say the teacher tells them, "Take off your hat, pick up your homework folder and take your seat in the reading circle." Your child gets their hat off, retrieves their homework folder, and then looks around as if they are lost. It's not because they weren't paying attention. It's not because they're not trying to cooperate. It's simply that that information has gone. Their working memory didn't hold onto it. The rest of the instructions have just disappeared.

Teachers are taught to avoid this by breaking things down into little steps. "Take your hat off," and then wait. "Pick up your homework folder," and then wait. And on it goes.

Accommodations, curriculum modifications, compensatory strategies are all the old way. Their purpose is to bypass the cognitive processes that are weak to minimize the impact. While they may be necessary to enable your child to make some sort of progress in school, they are crutches that don't improve your child's capacity to learn. They also do not prepare your child for life as an adult.

The new way is the exact opposite. Developing their cognitive skills will let us throw away those crutches, or many of them, anyway. The new way targets those underlying processes and helps your child develop the skills they need, so they can use them instead of bypassing them.

PARENT KEY 14

Cognitive skills can be developed in a
comprehensive integrated system in
order to reduce or eliminate the need for
accommodations, curriculum modifications,
and compensatory strategies.

"My son's first-grade teacher noted two major gaps – his
ability to focus and his abstract thinking skills. We heard
about BrainWare SAFARI and decided to give it a try. At
first, my son was frustrated. My wife worked with him on
Rhythm Ribbet, just listening to the beat. A few minutes

later, he ran into the kitchen screaming, 'I did it! I did it!' About two days later, he was working on BrainWare SAFARI, and he leaned forward in the chair, and his entire expression would change. We had never seen this before from him."

—Matt H., father of a seven-year-old boy with autism

THE NEW WAY

What is the New Way? If the old way is to bypass the cognitive processes that are weak in order to minimize the impact of processing deficits, the new way is the exact opposite. The new way is to target those underlying processes and help our children develop them to the point that they can use them instead of bypassing them.

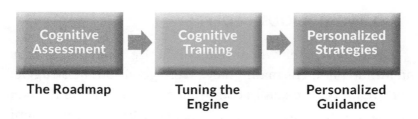

Cognitive Assessment ➡ Cognitive Training ➡ Personalized Strategies

The Roadmap · Tuning the Engine · Personalized Guidance

Figure 14. The new way approach to strengthening and integrating cognitive skills.

It starts with the kind of cognitive assessment we described in Chapters 2 and 3. This creates a clear picture of a child's cognitive strengths and weaknesses. You can see where the gaps are and what's already strong to build on. This is like having a roadmap – or even better – a GPS to make it clear where we are, where we're going, and how to get there.

The next component is comprehensive, integrated cognitive training. What most parents and schools don't know is that cognitive skills can be trained. It's like tuning the parts of an engine so that they all run smoothly and in sync. A well-tuned engine doesn't let us down when we need our working memory, visualization, or processing speed. The skills become automatic – it's almost like having a self-driving car – all these critical processes just work together.

And lastly, the roadmap and the newly tuned engine create a new pathway – a new plan of personalized learning designed uniquely for each child. This is a plan that takes advantage of a child's unique mind – like finding the genius in each child – because those special abilities are there – they need to be identified and developed.

What can happen when we don't understand a student's cognitive profile and what changes when we do? First, let's consider the case of Geoffrey, a real student (but not his real name).

SO, WHAT ABOUT GEOFFREY?

Geoffrey was ten when we met him. He aspired to become an airline pilot. His math grades were good. But he struggled with reading, especially comprehension, which he disliked and had to be pushed to do. When Geoffrey took his cognitive assessment, and we reviewed the results with his parents, Geoffrey's spatial perception was a strength (he scored at the 91st percentile). His verbal reasoning score was an exceptional weakness (he scored at the 3rd percentile). His other scores were in the expected range for his peer group.

Spatial perception involves:

- Perceiving and reasoning with visual-spatial information,

- Manipulating and rotating objects in space, and

- Determining how they relate to each other.

Verbal reasoning involves:

• Understanding relationships among words and language-based ideas,

• Reading between the lines,

• Making predictions and the like when information is presented in words.

It shouldn't be surprising that a student with low verbal reasoning capacity struggles with reading comprehension. But what if we didn't have this information about Geoffrey?

To his teacher, Geoffrey appeared lazy or uncooperative when it came to English Language Arts (ELA) assignments. He seemed bright and capable in so many areas. Indeed, his scores on all areas of the cognitive assessment were in the middle of the expected range or higher, except verbal reasoning. It makes sense that it is tough for the teacher to imagine why Geoffrey can't interpret a text or write more than a couple of basic sentences when he can solve complex math problems.

At home, Geoffrey's mother became quickly frustrated trying to help her son, while his father seemed to have more success. Was this a matter of personalities? Not at all. As we discussed the kind of help Geoffrey got from each parent, it became clear that mom (an attorney and someone with obviously strong verbal reasoning skills) used her strengths to try to explain the material. Dad, on the other hand, who shared strong spatial-reasoning skills with Geoffrey, was more effective because he tended to draw pictures. But each was helping based on their own cognitive strengths, not realizing why one was more effective than the other.

In school, Geoffrey's teachers have classes full of students. Some of those students have reading comprehension scores that look a lot like Geoffrey's, but that's really all they can see. Teachers are pushed to get their lagging students up to par to take the annual state assessment. In turn, they urge their students to apply themselves, work harder, and they give them more of the same kind of practice that failed to help these students succeed the first time. This might be the kind of school that blames the teachers for failing to engage in evidence-based instructional practices. Or it might be the kind of school that tells the parents that Geoffrey is not performing to his potential. He simply needs to work harder. There are, of course, many other kinds of schools, but those two reactions are very typical.

There is good news in Geoffrey's case. He received two things most students don't get. The first is highly personalized learning strategies that help him use his strong skills to improve reading comprehension. Creating a Mind Map is one of the learning strategies that helped transform his ability to comprehend the complexities and relationships among ideas in what he read. Mind Maps enable him to use his visual memory (which was stronger than his verbal memory) to recall the information. When he used the Mind Map as the basis for writing or to then verbally explain, he used it to develop his verbal reasoning. True personalization is not just about the "what" (what a student needs to learn or the gaps in their knowledge). It is about the "how."

The second was Geoffrey's participation in our cognitive training program to build his cognitive capacity comprehensively (forty-three cognitive skills, see Appendix 1) and in an integrated way. Following twelve weeks of training using BrainWare SAFARI, Geoffrey's score on the verbal reasoning portion of his cognitive test increased from the 3rd percentile to the 46th percentile. This moved from an exceptional weakness to the middle of the expected range.

When students struggle with learning, very often, it is not a matter of curriculum or instruction. Instead, the underlying reason is more likely a weakness in one or more cognitive skills.

"My daughter was coached through BrainWare SAFARI this past fall. Her coach was amazing and very patient and good at encouraging her. Her memory is much better now. She has acquired several skills that will be useful not just in schoolwork but also in daily living (even in making Nintendo games easier for her). We found BrainWare SAFARI to be a valuable resource for helping with challenges that having dyslexia has manifested. Thank you so much for the opportunity for her to do that."

—Jeanne M., mother of Faith (age thirteen)

■ Cognitive Training

Cognitive training (which is also sometimes called brain training) involves activities designed specifically to strengthen one or more cognitive skills. Some cognitive training programs focus on individual cognitive skills, while others are more comprehensive and integrated. They may be computer-based or use paper-and-pencil activities or a variety of other approaches.

While people participate in cognitive training for various reasons, the most common reason for children to be in a cognitive training program is to improve their capacity to learn.

We've been encountering the term "cognitive capacity"

more and more often since we started to make the distinction between "cognitive ability" and "cognitive capacity" several years ago. This distinction is important because every individual is born with the ability to develop cognitive skills. Cognitive capacity is different; it refers to how well those cognitive skills have already been developed.

Cognitive training has some things in common with physical training and physical exercise. A physical training program builds strength, speed, flexibility and stamina, all aspects of our bodies' capacity for physical activity. Effective cognitive training programs do the same thing for our brains' capacity for mental activity.

There is often confusion about the difference between cognitive training and brain games. The world is full of games, puzzles, software and other activities that involve mental processes. But most are intended for entertainment rather than meaningful impact on learning capacity. For a cognitive training program to have a significant impact, it needs to be designed according to specific neuroscience principles. By significant impact, we mean that it happens rapidly, is long-lasting and translates (generalizes) to academic work and everyday life.

Cognitive training must take a multi-disciplinary approach to have lasting, meaningful results. Integrating the best practices from clinical and educational psychology, auditory and vision developmental therapy, occupational therapy, speech and language pathology, neurology, and others builds a foundation for the right kind of cognitive training. No single discipline knows everything about how the human brain works. Combining the best information from all of these areas of expertise is the cornerstone of effective cognitive training, and that is how BrainWare SAFARI cognitive training software used in our programs was designed.

NEUROSCIENCE PRINCIPLES FOR EFFECTIVE COGNITIVE TRAINING

PRINCIPLE 1: NEUROPLASTICITY

The general term for the brain's ability to change and develop in response to its environment and the demands being placed on it is "neuroplasticity." Essentially, our brains develop by organizing themselves, creating and pruning neural pathways, connections, and networks in response to the environment and our individual experience.

Brain development and specific patterns of neural connections are not genetically predetermined in the way that attributes like red hair or blue eyes are determined. While our genetic code guides the development of intellect and learning ability, intellect and learning ability arise in significant part through the process of development. The brain's plasticity is greater in children, but the brain exhibits the ability to change and develop throughout life.

PRINCIPLE 2: AUTOMATICITY

When a certain set of steps or processes are performed repeatedly, the processes no longer require conscious thought to execute (like riding a bike or driving to a familiar location) and become automatic. Our brains can only perform one skill consciously at a time. When multiple cognitive skills are required, as in most learning situations, all but one of those skills must be performed automatically, at the non-conscious level.

When a skill becomes automatic and does not require conscious thought, an individual can perform that skill at the same time as other skills. Basic skills, like shifting attention, keeping information in a sequence, and visual span must function automatically to free up conscious thought for other activities, like listening, comparing, deciding, planning, drawing conclusions and the like.

PRINCIPLE 3: INTEGRATION (CROSS-TRAINING)

Not only do cognitive skills need to be strong, but they also need to work together. Two recent research studies have made this clear. Researchers at the National University, Galway, concluded that the efficiency of connections across and between parts of the brain was more indicative of intelligence than functioning within discrete parts of the brain.[11]

Scientists at the University of Cambridge came up with similar results when looking at learning disabilities.[12] They found that brain differences did not map onto any labels that the children in the study had been given, including ADHD, ASD (autism spectrum disorder), SLD, and others. Instead, the connections among hubs or networks across the brain were the best predictors of how learning happened. The researchers concluded that labels are of little use in helping children and recommended an approach focused on areas of cognitive strengths and weaknesses rather than a diagnosis.

---

11 Holleran, L., *et al.*, The Relationship Between White Matter Microstructure and General Cognitive Ability in Patients With Schizophrenia and Healthy Participants in the ENIGMA Consortium. *American Journal of Psychiatry*; 26 Mar 2020. doi.org/10.1176/appi.ajp.2019.19030225.

12 Siugzdaite, R. et al. Transdiagnostic brain mapping in developmental disorders. *Current Biology*; 27 Feb 2020. doi.org/10.1016/j.cub.2020.01.078

The implications of this new research are important. It means that cognitive processes are more relevant than diagnoses to support a struggling learner. Any effort to improve cognitive functioning must take a whole-brain approach to ensure that cognitive processes work together efficiently.

PRINCIPLE 4: PROGRESSIVE CHALLENGE

Cognitive development occurs at the outer edges of our competence. Therefore, sequenced challenges that address the range of each individual's strengths and weaknesses are required to provide the appropriate levels of challenge and intensity. If a task is too far above our current state of development, we will become frustrated and give up. If tasks are too easy, we become bored. The optimal level of challenge is sometimes called the Zone of Proximal Development. Making sure that a child is working in their Zone of Proximal Development is simply "meeting them where they are."

Delivering an appropriate sequence of challenges results in "smart practice" (intense and rewarding repetition). Truly effective cognitive training programs avoid predictable progression that causes the brain to lose interest and engage with less intensity.

PRINCIPLE 5: FREQUENCY AND INTENSITY

Promises of meaningful cognitive change in five minutes a day or usage for a couple of weeks are not credible. To have a significant impact on cognitive skills in a way that is lasting and transfers to academics and everyday activities, a cognitive training program typically requires a usage protocol of three to five times a week, in thirty to sixty-minute sessions for three months or more.

PRINCIPLE 6: FEEDBACK

Immediate feedback is necessary to enable error correction and faster, more accurate learning. Rapid feedback also enables more repetitions in a given amount of time. For this reason, technology is becoming an increasingly important part of cognitive training. In addition to the feedback provided in a computer-based video-game format, there is evidence that success in a video game releases dopamine, which is involved in learning and feelings of reward.

Human coaching is another important aspect of feedback. The most effective cognitive training includes a coach, just as a personal trainer enhances physical training.

PRINCIPLE 7: ENGAGEMENT

Stimulation is an important factor in motivating attention and meaningful participation in learning activities. In fact, the science and education communities are increasingly recognizing the value of digital game-based learning. The compelling characteristics of good video games motivate initial engagement with a challenging activity. They can help sustain motivation as the challenge progresses. Persistence inspired by a feedback loop reinforces and supports the brain's natural mechanisms that reward us for accomplishing something challenging.

What happens when we apply neuroscience principles in a comprehensive cognitive training program? Learning becomes less effortful, even joyful. We strengthen instructional effectiveness along with the brain, the command center of the nervous system, in the ways the brain learns best.

PARENT KEY 15

We are not stuck with the cognitive skills we have. Cognitive skills can be developed with the right kind of cognitive training. Not all cognitive training is created equal. The training must embody the principles of neuroplasticity, automaticity, integration (cross-training), progressive challenge, frequency and intensity, feedback and engagement in order to develop an individual's cognitive skills comprehensively and in a way that they all work effectively together. This is how BrainWare SAFARI was built.

Cognitive Growth for the Sixty Not-So-Average Students

In the last chapter, we shared data on sixty students who participated in our programs and their percentile rankings on the cognitive assessment they took at the start. The following charts show both their pre-test and their post-test percentile rankings (before and after their cognitive training).

Average Cognitive Scores Pre- and Post-

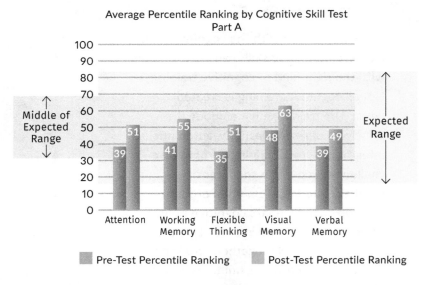

Figures 15a and b. Average pre- and post-test cognitive skill rankings for sixty students.

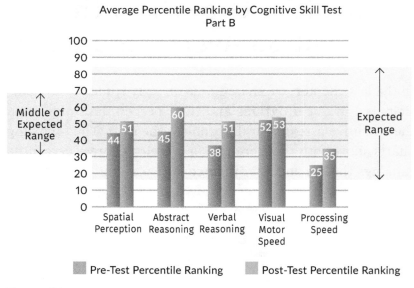

Figure 15b.

As you can see in the chart, cognitive skills improved across the board in multiple areas. After completing our comprehensive, integrated cognitive training program, students had average scores in all cognitive areas within the middle of the expected range.

But remember that these were students with very uneven cognitive skills. What about those weaker areas? What happened to those?

The next charts display just those skills that were below the expected range on the pre-test.

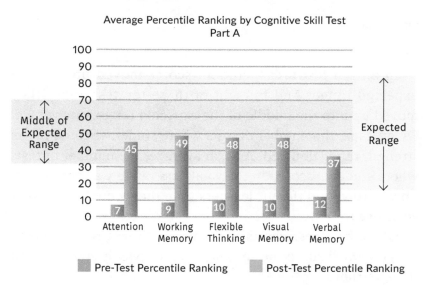

Figures 16a and b. Average percentile ranking pre- and post-test scores, impact on scores below middle of expected range.

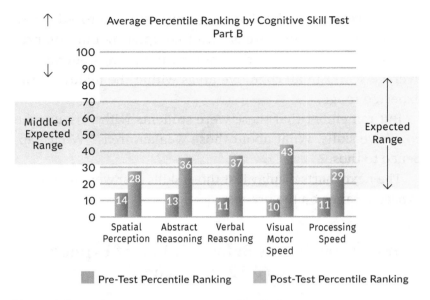

Figure 16b.

In all ten test areas, student scores moved up into the expected range. And in eight of those ten test areas, they moved up into the middle of the expected range, on average. On average, the number of tests where students scored in the strength range doubled. And on average, the number of tests where students scored in the weakness range was cut in half. These are very different learners than they were before their cognitive training.

Of course, these charts again display averages. In the next chapter, we'll share the stories of some specific students and their journeys.

These results are just one example of what we have seen over years of examining the impact of cognitive training with BrainWare SAFARI. Reports of peer-reviewed research, field studies in schools, and case studies are available on our website at https://mybrainware.com/blog/category/research/.

◼ Students with Specific Learning Disabilities (SLD)

SLD is one of those "labels" – a diagnosis that means a child has been determined to have a learning disability that qualifies them for an IEP. SLD relates specifically to deficits in psychological or cognitive processes. For this study[13], students with SLD were randomly assigned to two groups. One group was a control group. They just received their normal instruction and supports. The second group participated in cognitive training using BrainWare SAFARI in addition to their normal instruction and supports.

The BrainWare group engaged in cognitive training three to five times per week, for thirty to forty-five minutes each time, for twelve weeks. The students took cognitive and academic tests beforehand and at the end of twelve weeks. For the students in the control group, no significant cognitive change was noted. In contrast, the students who participated in cognitive training, on average, closed the cognitive gap almost to the level of normally developing students.

Their cognitive gains also translated into greater academic gains. The control group students experienced incremental progress, as such students usually do. Students in the cognitive training group gained 0.8 grade equivalent in reading and 1.0 grade equivalent in math over twelve weeks. That equates to a 31 percent improvement in reading proficiency and a 28 percent improvement in math proficiency.

---

13 Sarah Abitbol Avtzon. Effect of Neuroscience-Based Cognitive Skill Training on Growth of Cognitive Deficits Associated with Learning Disabilities in Children Grades 2 to 4. *Learning Disabilities: A Multidisciplinary Journal*, v18 n3 p111-122 Fall 2012.

Students with Specific Learning Disabilities (SLD) Pre/Post Cognitive Training

90% Is Expected RPI of Normally Developing Student

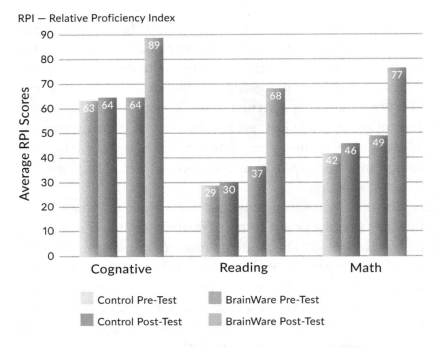

Figure 17. Impact of cognitive skills development for students with learning disabilities.

Students Behind in Reading

In a study with students who were one or more grade levels behind in reading, twelve weeks of cognitive training with BrainWare SAFARI resulted in multiple grade-level changes in basic academic skills, as shown in the following chart.

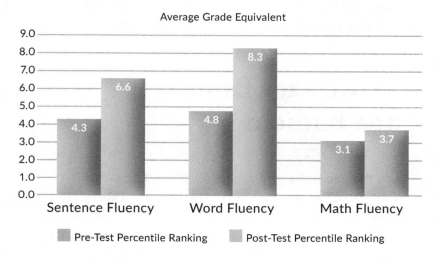

Figure 18. Improvement in academic test scores for students behind in reading.

The students, on average, also gained 2.5 times the number of reading levels (Fountas and Pinnell) expected during that twelve-week period (4.1 compared to 1.5 reading levels). One student improved ten reading levels in twelve weeks.

Increase in Students Qualifying for Gifted Programs

The year after South Carolina changed the process and criteria for students to participate in a gifted program, no students at one elementary school qualified. Following cognitive training with BrainWare SAFARI, 94 percent of the students improved their scores on the CogAT(Cognitive Abilities Test, the test used to qualify students for the gifted program). Ten percent of the students qualified for the gifted program, and another 5 percent scored well enough to participate in further screening.

■ A Message from Anne Budicin

Ann Budicin is the principal of Glenwood Academy in Glenwood, Illinois, a school that serves students from economically disadvantaged backgrounds who often have complicated family situations. She brings her experience as a resource teacher and her strong skills in special education, program development, instructional planning, and team building to her role and to create a strong, supportive community at Glenwood.

BrainWare SAFARI is a way to improve your cognitive processing skills. It's presented in a game format that's fun and challenging, and it's fun for kids of all ages. It appeals to our second graders and our eighth graders. It is the one program that really addresses thinking skills and really helps students become better learners.

I'm really impressed with how it addresses attention. We have several children with ADHD, and none of them are taking medication. So, we were looking for ways to help them focus and help them become better learners. BrainWare really addresses that in the games and the opportunities it provides for focus.

The students that come to Glenwood often are several years behind age expectancy in auditory processing skills. I've taught Resource for several years. It's tough to find programs that work in addressing those skills and helping those kids really close those gaps in the processing areas. BrainWare does a great job addressing those issues. It's enjoyable in that every time you pass a level, your animal grows up. The students find it's so exciting to see what's going to happen next!

Let me tell you about this one student. He came to us as a second grader, about to be placed in a self-contained room for developmentally delayed children. When we tested him, we realized that he really had an above-average IQ but struggled in the processing areas. It was really exciting because we could put him on BrainWare, and we could work on those skills and really help him achieve his potential. He was by no means a slow learner, but he had some gaps in his processing skills. BrainWare really enabled him to close those gaps.

BrainWare is challenging, but it's fun for the kids. They feel like they're playing a video game like they do at home. They want to pass the levels – they're very enthused about passing those levels! The students look forward to coming and doing BrainWare. In fact, our study group doing it every day for thirty minutes for the whole quarter are disappointed the quarter is almost over. They're like, "We want to keep doing BrainWare! It's real fun when you get it."

Answers to the Nonverbal Reasoning Puzzles

- Abstract Reasoning Puzzle: The answer is C.
- Shape Rotation Puzzle: The answer is

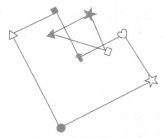

CHAPTER FIVE

Step #4   Move Beyond Grit

"Once you start, you've just got to go through. You can't just like give up in the middle of it. I felt like I won a Nobel Peace Prize. It was such an accomplishment! It was so hard, and I finally did it. I did it! Like wow! It was amazing. It seems easy for a lot of the games, and then you get to the last level, and you think you can't do it. It was super exciting to completely master the whole thing."

—Student at Pope John Paul II Catholic School,
Lecanto, FL

◼ It's Confidence They Need, Not Grit

The concept of "grit" has quite a following. It is implicit in the saying, "The difference between winners and losers is that winners don't give up." The idea that grit is the determining factor for success became even more popular when Angela Duckworth published her book called, simply, *Grit*. She characterized grit as a combination of perseverance and passion. The notion is that there is some strong incentive (passion), particularly in the long-term, that helps students persist in the face of adversity.

Duckworth's work has been interpreted as implying that students need to develop grit, by finding their passion and just working hard. And if hard work doesn't pay off right away, they just need to work harder. Essentially, the message to students has been, "Try harder. Try again. Remember your goal. Don't give up. Get some grit."

When students don't do what teachers want them to do, when they want them to do it, it can produce a variety of reactions. Teachers see a kid who isn't complying and may see opposition. Teachers see a student who can't get started on their work and may see laziness. Teachers see a student who gets frustrated with a task and gives up quickly and may see a "lack of grit."

There are a couple of problems with the grit approach. First, grit and effort are internal, not things that can always be accurately gauged by a parent or teacher. In fact, teachers and parents misinterpret kids' behaviors all the time.

A recent conversation with a family started with this statement, "Juana's school just called and told us that they think she has Oppositional Defiant Disorder (ODD). That's just crazy. She's a sweet kid and always wants to do what's right. What are they talking about?"

Juana did not have Oppositional Defiant Disorder. What we learned from her cognitive assessment is that she had slow processing speed. It took her longer than her peers to process, understand and respond to something being asked of her. Her teachers and other school staff, who didn't have that information, and didn't understand what slow processing speed might look like in a classroom, assumed that Juana must be intentionally uncooperative and simply unwilling to comply.

Parents, grandparents and teachers usually have some opinions when they look at the list of cognitive skills in Appendix 1 on which skills are stronger or weaker. And those can be very helpful indicators. But it is the cognitive assessment process that uncovers what we really need to know about a child's cognitive strengths and weaknesses.

PARENT KEY 16

Cognitive skills are the root cause of many behavior issues as well as learning issues. Often parents and teachers misinterpret a child's behavior because they don't know what cognitive skills are involved.

Another problem with the concept of grit is that it implies that the only thing needed to accomplish one's goals is to keep doing the same thing over and over again. And that – doing the same thing over and over again and expecting a different result – has come to be defined as insanity.

Now, no parent or teacher would intentionally encourage their student to engage in insane behavior, but when a teacher or a parent misinterprets a child's struggles as laziness, then telling a child just to work harder, just to get some grit, is really the same thing.

Still, we know that giving up doesn't lead to success either. So, what is it that we and our children need?

We have a lot of words for what it takes to do hard things and overcome obstacles. Grit, perseverance, fortitude, tenacity, resilience, persistence, stick-to-it-iveness, backbone, pluck, moral fiber, stamina, spunk …

What we have come to understand is that the almost magical part of the 5 Steps is that children learn persistence as they strengthen their cognitive skills because they develop confidence. It's confidence they need, not grit. When a child's learning capacity is strong, their skills are there for them. They don't have to just bear down and hope they can tackle the problem. They KNOW they have the skills to do it. They move beyond grit.

Grit is what you need when all you can do is grind it out. It's what you need when you don't know if you can do something.

It's about trying again and again, trying harder, without having any real belief that you can do it.

When you know you can do something, you move beyond grit to – *confidence.*

Let's take a look at a few students who moved beyond grit to confidence.

CASE STUDY: BELLA

Bella was thirteen years old and in the eighth grade. She was being educated at home. Her parents told us, and we can confirm that she has a great imagination and is amazingly creative. But schoolwork was often a real struggle for her. It would take her a long time to complete her assignments. She was reading below grade level and often had problems understanding what she read. She had a dyslexia diagnosis. Other concerns were anxiety, auditory processing and fine motor skills. She often struggled with staying focused.

One part of the initial assessment we do involves parents filling out a cognitive rating scale.

And by the way, the rating scales (for different ages) are free and available on our website at https://mybrainware. com/brainware-cognitive-rating-scales/.

When Bella's parents completed the rating scale, the areas of greatest concern were the difficulties she had with the following skills:

ATTENTION

- Sustaining attention for an appropriate period of time
- Paying attention to details

MEMORY

- Remembering how to do a task days or weeks after learning it
- Repeating information she has just received

PERCEPTUAL PROCESSING

- Following a map

EXECUTIVE FUNCTIONS

- Handling complex tasks that require significant mental effort without getting frustrated
- Having confidence in her learning abilities

Frustration and lack of confidence go hand in hand with learning struggles.

Another part of the initial assessment involves a nationally normed scientifically valid assessment of ten cognitive skills, as we have discussed earlier in the book. As you may already have noticed, ten cognitive skills are fewer cognitive skills than the full complement of forty-three skills developed in BrainWare SAFARI. Since it is not realistic or necessary to assess every skill to demonstrate cognitive growth, the ten skills assessed represent some of the most important skills that can be measured in an online assessment.

On her initial assessment, Bella showed a strength in visual-motor speed and weaknesses in several skills. Her other skills were in the expected range (typical for her peer group – for those with a math bent, within one standard deviation of the mean).

Bella's Initial Cognitive Assessment Scores

Cognitive Strengths	Skills in Expected Range	Cognitive Weaknesses
Visual-Motor Speed	Attention Working Memory Flexible Thinking Visual Memory Verbal Memory Spatial Perception Abstract Reasoning	Verbal Reasoning* Processing Speed**

*Verbal Reasoning: The ability to understand and logically work through concepts and problems presented in words. Weaker verbal reasoning is related to difficulty drawing inferences, understanding and using figurative (non-literal) language.

**Processing Speed: The ability to scan, inspect and compare incoming auditory and visual information.

Bella's low verbal reasoning score and her slow processing speed especially stood out.

Now it was clear that "Bella's" struggles with reading and math word problems had an underlying cognitive explanation. And unless these weaker cognitive areas could be addressed, it was almost certain that she would continue to struggle in those areas.

But we know that, with the right kind of cognitive training, these skills can be developed. Twelve weeks later, after her cognitive training program, Bella took the assessment again.

So how much of an impact did the cognitive training program that we provided for Bella have?

This time Flexible Thinking, Abstract Reasoning, and Visual Memory had all moved into the strength range. Everything else that had been a weakness was now well within the expected range.

Bella's Post-Training Cognitive Assessment Scores

Cognitive Strengths	Skills in Expected Range	Cognitive Weaknesses
Visual-Motor Speed	Attention	None
Visual Memory	Working Memory	
Abstract Reasoning	Flexible Thinking	
	Verbal Memory	
	Spatial Perception	
	Verbal Reasoning	
	Processing Speed	

It's funny what Bella noticed about her cognitive growth following her twelve weeks of training. Of course, it can be hard to notice changes in ourselves because we live in our own brains all the time. Bella's first thought was that she remembered where she put her hairbrush. And then she said, "I feel more awake." If we think for a moment about what feeling more awake means, it makes total sense in the context of her improved attention and processing speed. Being able to focus and sustain attention and to respond more quickly add up to feeling more alert.

And when asked about school, she said things "just seem easier." Bella's confidence in her learning skills soared.

CASE STUDY: EVAN

Evan was nine and going into the fourth grade. Evan's mother knew he was bright, but he had been diagnosed with ADHD, and anxiety was a major concern. He struggled to get started on assignments. He'd become frustrated to the point of tears. When he'd get stuck on an assignment, it took him a very long time to get his work done. His mother was a teacher and knew he needed something other than what he was getting in school.

When Evan's mother completed the rating scale, the areas of greatest concern were:

ATTENTION

- Sustaining attention for an appropriate period of time
- Maintaining proper attention even when distractions are present
- Paying attention to details

MEMORY

- Remembering how to do a task days or weeks after learning it

SELF-ESTEEM

- Bouncing back from failures or setbacks quickly
- Enjoying taking on challenging tasks

Then came Evan's cognitive assessment.

Evan's Initial Cognitive Assessment Scores

Cognitive Strengths	Skills in Expected Range	Cognitive Weaknesses
Verbal Reasoning	Attention Working Memory Flexible Thinking* Verbal Memory Visual Memory Abstract Reasoning Spatial Perception	Visual-Motor Speed** Processing Speed***

***Flexible Thinking:** The abiily to change our mindset when the rules of the world around us change, to shift between mental processes.

**Visual-Motor Speed: The ability to use the eyes and hands together efficiently, as in writing, drawing, typing, catching a ball, etc.

******Processing Speed:** The ability to scan, inspect and compare incoming auditory and visual information.

Unlike, Bella who really struggled with verbal reasoning, this was an area of strength for Evan. However, Evan's slower processing speed meant that it would take him much longer to complete work than his peers. Slow visual-motor speed would make the physical aspects of writing and other tasks that require fine motor skills very challenging. And while Evan's Flexible Thinking Score was in the Expected Range, it was barely in that range. Weaker flexible thinking meant that, even though his reasoning skills were generally strong, he had some trouble adapting when his first approach to solving a problem didn't work.

It is not surprising that his learning challenges resulted in debilitating anxiety.

PARENT KEY 17

Kids with uneven cognitive skills often
have anxiety. Some learning experiences
are easy, and others are inexplicably hard.
They don't know why and can't predict
whether something will be easy or will
stump them. No wonder they're anxious.

Now let's look at the impact of BrainWare cognitive training
on Evan's cognitive skills.

Evan's Post-Training Cognitive Assessment Scores

Cognitive Strengths	Skills in Expected Range	Cognitive Weaknesses
Attention	Verbal Memory	None
Working Memory	Abstract Reasoning	
Flexible Thinking	Processing Speed	
Visual Memory		
Spatial Perception		
Verbal Reasoning		
Visual-Motor Speed		

As Evan's mother said, "Wow!" All of Evan's cognitive skills
were now well within the expected range, and most were significantly higher. Evan's ability to get his work done in an
appropriate amount of time soared, as did his self-confidence.
This is an extremely capable learner who was previously unable
to show what he could do because of some cognitive stumbling
blocks.

CASE STUDY: ROBERT

Robert was nine years old when he started in our program. He had been diagnosed with ADHD and dyslexia. He suffered from depression and resisted anything to do with school and school-work. Meltdowns were common.

When Robert's mother completed the rating scale, the areas of greatest concern were:

MEMORY

- Remembering to do things he was asked to do

PERCEPTUAL PROCESSING

- Working on schoolwork independently without much help
- Handling complex tasks requiring significant mental effort without getting frustrated
- Completing homework or other tasks that require mental effort in the appropriate amount of time

LIFE MANAGEMENT SKILLS

- Managing time effectively
- Is organized

SELF-ESTEEM

- Enjoying taking on challenging tasks
- Having confidence in his learning abilities

The areas of concern suggested a complex combination of cognitive weaknesses that would make learning a daunting task for this young man. And that is, in fact, what we saw in his cognitive assessment results.

Robert's Initial Cognitive Assessment Scores

Cognitive Strengths	Skills in Expected Range	Cognitive Weaknesses
None	Attention	Working Memory*
	Abstract Reasoning	Flexible Thinking**
	Spatial Perception	Visual Memory***
	Verbal Reasoning	Verbal Memory+
	Visual-Motor Speed	Processing Seed++

*__Working Memory:__ The ability to hold and manipulate information consciously in the mind.

**__Flexible Thinking:__ The ability to change our mindset when the rules of the world around us change, to shift between mental processes.

***__Visual Memory:__ The ability to store and retrieve visual information (images, charts, etc.).

+__Verbal Memory:__ The ability to store and retrieve information in words (read or heard).

++__Processing Speed:__ The ability to scan, inspect and compare incoming auditory and visual information.

You will see the word "none" above for cognitive strengths for Robert. This requires some clarification. Just to be clear, Robert did have relative cognitive strengths and stronger areas to build on, just like every child does. And when we work with parents and children, we always start with and focus on those strengths. The "none" in this context means that his test scores on the pre-test fell in the expected range and below.

It is not surprising to see low scores were in multiple areas. It required so much mental effort for Robert to stay focused, shift gears mentally, and hold information in his mind while he was doing a task, that it exhausted him.

The fact that memory for both visual and verbal information was so low meant that committing information to memory and recalling it later would be very difficult and would suggest poor performance on most academic tasks.

And to make learning even more difficult, it would take Robert far longer than his peers to complete most academic tasks.

Robert went through fourteen weeks of cognitive training (three times a week) and took the cognitive assessment again.

Robert's Post-Training Cognitive Assessment Scores

Cognitive Strengths	Skills in Expected Range	Cognitive Weaknesses
Verbal Reasoning	Attention Flexible Thinking Abstract Reasoning Spatial Perception Verbal Memory Visual Memory Visual-Motor Speed Processing Speed	Working Memory

After comprehensive, integrated cognitive training, all but one of Robert's ten scores were now within the expected range or higher. His Verbal Reasoning reached the strength range, and his Attention score had almost reached that range, as well. His working memory capacity improved but remained in the weakness range. He will still need support, but that support can now be very targeted because his other skills are so much stronger.

PARENT KEY 18

Our brains use 20 percent of the energy consumed in our bodies, proportionately much more than any other part of the body. Difficult or complex mental tasks require a lot more energy than we realize.

Following his cognitive training, Robert's mother rated him as average or above average for all the behaviors associated with cognitive skills in the rating scale – a remarkable change in the short time of fourteen weeks.

And what it shows is what happens when we can help a child strengthen skills in a way that lets their true strengths shine. Robert wasn't able to show what he could do. Now learning and demonstrating what he can accomplish are not nearly as challenging, and Robert has the self-confidence he needs to succeed. Grit couldn't do it. Confidence, built on stronger learning capacity, could and did.

The transformations that occurred for Bella, Evan, and Robert would never have happened if their parents hadn't Taken the Wheel and Set Higher Expectations and Built the Cognitive Foundation for their children's learning. That gave them the confidence that they needed.

So, Step #4 is to move beyond grit. It's time to use new tools to deal with the underlying cause and not the symptoms. When a child's learning capacity is strong, their skills are just there for them. They don't have to bear down and hope and pray that they can tackle the problem. They know they have the skills to do it.

The following conversations demonstrate how kids recognize the difference when they know they can be successful because of strengthened cognitive skills.

■ A Message from Peter Kline

The late Peter Kline was a renowned educator and author
of many books, including *The Everyday Genius* and *Why
America's Children Can't Think.* He has spoken with many
students about learning and about the changes they
experienced following their comprehensive, integrated
cognitive training program. (As background, Slithering
Symbols and Crocodile Recollection are two of the twenty
exercises in BrainWare SAFARI.)

CHARLOTTE: Slithering Symbols and Crocodile Recollection
were kind of hard for me, and I couldn't pass the levels.
But one day, I just passed the levels and went up to maybe
the fifth level, just like magic! I didn't really know how
I could do that, but maybe it was because I had stopped
doing those exercises for a while.

PETER KLINE: Sometimes when something is hard for you
and you keep trying and trying and trying, and then you
go to sleep or forget about it for a while, your brain puts
it together for you and then you can do it right. That's
what you were experiencing. Suddenly it got easy when
it seemed impossible. Does that make you think that you
might be pretty good at doing other difficult things?

CHARLOTTE: Yeah.

PETER KLINE: I bet you are.

HENRY: I got much better at listening. I used to misunderstand stuff sometimes. I'd just go ahead and work on the work but didn't even do the instructions. I guess I just wanted it done.

PETER KLINE: So, you'd just zip through it.

HENRY: Yeah.

PETER KLINE: And BrainWare won't let you get away with that. You have to go at a certain pace, so it's teaching you how to pace your work, so you're certain of success.

HENRY: Yeah, it taught me to slow down and like double-check.

PETER KLINE: You know, if every student did that, do you know what would happen to the average grades in people's classes?

HENRY: We'd get better.

PETER KLINE: That's right! They would skyrocket.

Peter wrote the following explanation of the importance of cognitive skills,

> Information is growing at a pace never before seen in the history of the world. Our children and grandchildren are growing up in a world where they'll have to deal with problems we haven't thought about. BrainWare SAFARI is one of the tools that can make that experience delightful instead of frightening and threatening.

◼ Beyond Grit Is a Growth Mindset

Just like the word "grit" has multiple synonyms, so does the currently popular term "growth mindset." Flexibility, adaptability, zeal, willingness, a positive outlook, resilience, motivation. We have a lot of words for what it takes to learn from mistakes and try something new when our first approach doesn't work.

A growth mindset – or its opposite, a fixed mindset – refers to our unconscious attitudes about intelligence. Someone with a growth mindset believes that intelligence and talents are developed. Someone with a fixed mindset believes that intelligence and talents are something we are born with, and there's nothing much we can do about them. Of course, these are extremes, and people are generally somewhere on a continuum between the two.

You probably know many people with a predominantly fixed mindset, and perhaps you have some fixed mindset tendencies yourself. It's common to see a talented musician or an elite athlete, or a wealthy businessperson and assume that they are different from us. They must have some innate, God-given, pre-existing talent that they were born with. And it is true, at least partially. Intelligence is partly genetic (programmed), but it develops in interaction with the environment so it can change. And it can change a lot.

Comprehensive cognitive training that integrates cognitive processes is one thing that can dramatically enhance cognitive skills (the components of intelligence). Still, there are other things we can do as parents that can have a tremendous impact on the mindset our children bring to school and to the tasks and activities they engage in at home and in the outside world.

The concept of a Growth Mindset comes from the work of Dr. Carol Dweck at Stanford.[14] The research is clear. Individuals with a growth mindset – that is, who believe that intelligence and talent can be developed – do better than those who think that talent is innate and that intelligence doesn't change much. We are better off if we have a growth mindset, and certainly, our children will be, as well. Interestingly, just because a parent has a growth mindset doesn't mean that their children will. It is important to understand what fosters a growth mindset for ourselves and also for our children.

Mindset isn't just about what you say. It is how you process feedback and how you interact with your child. If asked, many people would say that they have a growth mindset – after all, it's critical for parents. But how you really behave, what you say, and what you believe at a nonconscious level can be different.

Here's a concrete example from Betsy.

I believe strongly that intelligence, reasoning skills and talents can be developed. That's what we help people do every day. But I am still tempted to say to one of my sons or one of my granddaughters, "Boy, are you smart."

What happens when you tell a child that they are smart? It reinforces the concept that kids often have that they are either smart or dumb. If you ask, any kid will give you a list of the smart kids in their class at school. If kids who are smart do well in school, it is because they are smart, or that's what most kids

---

14 Carol S. Dewck, Ph.D., *MINDSET: The New Psychology of Success*, (New York: Ballantine Books, 2016).

assume. And kids who do poorly in school do so because they aren't smart, they believe. That's a fixed mindset.

With that belief structure, working hard at something challenging becomes something kids avoid. If something is hard, it means I'm not smart. Therefore, I shouldn't even try because if I fail, it means I'm not smart. Telling a child that they're smart can really backfire. It can result in them actually resisting taking on more challenging activities.

How often have you heard your child say something like, "This is too hard. I can't do it. I'm just dumb." How often have you said or thought that yourself? A growth mindset seems like it would be easy, but it's a deceptively simple concept.

A growth mindset uses or implies one of the most powerful words in the English language (and every human language has its equivalent) – the word YET.

YET contains within it the promise of accomplishments we can't yet imagine. It contains within it a vision of our future selves doing exactly what we have just failed at – and doing it successfully. And it gives appropriate value to a mistake and a learning experience.

When you find yourself saying or thinking, "This is too hard. I can't do it," add the word YET.

"This is hard. I can't do it yet."

"I needed this mistake to help me understand how to do it right." Yes, be thankful for the mistakes you make!

How we model a growth mindset and how we talk about mistakes and failure has a big impact. It changes how children develop a more growth-oriented or more fixed mindset. Creating a safe environment for children to make mistakes and learn from them is an essential part of this.

PARENT KEY 19

"Yet" is one of the most powerful words we can use to help our children develop a growth mindset. If they are struggling with something, they can get help, or they can try a different strategy. Whenever you hear your child (or yourself) saying, "I can't do this," immediately add the word "yet."

■ Getting to a Growth Mindset

When students struggle or fail, one of two things tends to happen:

1. When the going gets tough, the tough get going, or

2. When the going gets tough, forget it.

Teachers and parents can readily see these responses in action. It doesn't take brain scans for them to identify which category their students fall into. The question teachers and parents have struggled with, essentially forever, is what to do. Are these just descriptions of students, or can we influence how our students respond when the going gets tough?

"I remember when my mom told me about the program. At first, I was confused, but when I finally got into it, it made so much sense. It was fun. I barely even knew I was learning anything. I remember before BrainWare SAFARI, I was so

impatient. Waiting for a ride, I would feel like, when are we
gonna do this? Come on, let's do this. After doing the frog
game, where you had to wait to click and wait to click, now
I'm starting to be more patient. Even if you think you can't
beat it, if you take your time, you can beat it."

—Student at Christian Heritage Academy, Northfield, IL

The research on Growth Mindset emphasizes the value of
mistakes and supports the idea that some students are fueled
by failure and learn from their mistakes. They believe that
talent and intelligence can be developed.

Since the original publication of her book, Dweck has
emphasized that the focus in a Growth Mindset is not just an
effort, but an effort that tries different solutions when the first
approach doesn't work. It's about learning.

And it is that shift in mindset that happens when children
develop stronger cognitive skills. When they have the genuine
confidence to take on difficult tasks. When they know, without
question, that mistakes are an essential part of learning. When
their response to a mistake or a failure is to try again with a
shift in strategy. They know that intelligence can be developed
because that is what they have done. The lesson and belief
structure become internalized.

"The students absolutely loved it. They would get a little
bit frustrated more near the end when they got to the
higher levels, but they persevered. I found that they
helped each other. I think too assigning the games that
they had to play helped. Sometimes in the morning, if it

was a harder game, I'd hear, "Aah," but they knew they had their ten minutes, and they had to stick it out.

"I have heard from the teachers that the students who used the program last year are excellent workers, that they get right down to work. I haven't heard them say that before. The biggest thing for me was that they were very attentive."

—Teacher and BrainWare SAFARI Lead, Huron-Superior Catholic District School Board

As a parent, nurturing a Growth Mindset in your children increases the chances of success exponentially, so what can you do to encourage them in this direction?

WAYS TO DISCOURAGE A GROWTH MINDSET

Here are some statements that tend to reinforce a fixed mindset.

Wow, you're so smart. You aced that test and barely studied for it.

The implication here is that if you're smart, you don't have to study. And therefore, if you have to study, you aren't really very smart. Thinking this way discourages someone from even trying if something is hard because it can only prove that they're not really as bright as they've been told.

That's OK. Spelling isn't that important.

Minimizing the importance of something that is difficult leads to avoidance of learning opportunities that are challenging. Pretty soon, just about everything can become unimportant.

That teacher of yours sure picked some hard spelling words this week.

Blaming failure on someone else means that you don't have to think about what you could have done differently to be more successful. The essence of a growth mindset is figuring out a different approach to a task, adjusting a strategy, thinking about how to change.

Don't get down on yourself. You'll get it if you just keep trying.

This type of message is similar to telling someone they just need more grit. It is about repeating the same thing in the same way and expecting a different result. The key to a growth mindset is to ask what we can do to get a different result the next time.

WAYS TO NURTURE A GROWTH MINDSET

- Present skills as learnable.

- Convey that you value learning and understand what it takes to develop abilities.

- Convey that it doesn't all depend on innate talent.

- Give feedback that promotes learning and trying new strategies and approaches.

- Make it clear that you (and other adults and peers) are resources for learning. We will all help each other learn.

- Model your own growth mindset (I wonder what I can learn from that mistake/experience.)

- Teach about how the brain learns.

If making mistakes is essential to learning, then it's essential to let your child make mistakes along the way. If you step in so that they never make a mistake, they aren't learning the lesson they needed to learn from making that mistake.

And they're also getting the message from you that they really aren't competent. They still need you to act for them.

Now, remember that second facet, how your expectations will affect how you respond to struggles and setbacks your child may encounter. If your expectation is high, you will be more likely to seek out the resources they need to meet those expectations. That may mean being a strong champion for them at school to get the kinds of supports they need. It may mean arranging for them to take a special class, take on a project, whatever it may be that will nurture your child's strengths and help them push past their stumbling blocks.

Most parents share a common, deeply held belief that it is their job to raise their child to be an independent, self-sustaining, contributing member of the family, community, and society. Expecting that as an outcome, believing that it will happen if you do the right things, is a powerful predictor of children's success. If you believe, you work hard to support them in helping them develop. If you believe, they believe too.

"I think there's a lot of students that we see that are on the cusp. We can see that potential, and we can see where they have the potential to grow and learn. I think BrainWare can help move them over that cusp and help them progress in addition to the support that the school gives them. BrainWare SAFARI really aligns well because it's allowing them to expand their cognitive abilities, and that's what they have to be able to do to be higher-order thinkers.

"I also used the program SuccessMaker in my classroom. I think that it's a great program, and it helps the students, but it focuses more on the academic aspect helping them with reading and math skills. BrainWare SAFARI really benefits from the cognitive side, waking up different areas of their brain that might not have been used before. It helps them grow cognitively so they can handle higher-order thinking and more complex skills.

"I've been really impressed as I've seen firsthand how this program impacts our students here at Pope John Paul II, especially those who are struggling. I have one particular student, Mary, who started the year I started teaching here. I worked with her my first year here when she was in third grade. She really struggled with reading, decoding and comprehending. She did the BrainWare program this year, and she just blossomed! I saw how much it impacted her reading. This year, I said to her teacher that if I could give an award for the most improved student to one student, it would be her! She has genuinely become a reader this year. She is checking out books on her own, reading at home, and she's comprehending and understanding. She's really developed a love for reading, and I really feel that BrainWare SAFARI had a big impact on that. It helped her grow cognitively, so she's able to be the reader that she had the potential to be, but SAFARI really brought it out.

—Karen Keene, Title I Resource Teacher,
Citrus County Schools

The theory of neuroplasticity is no longer a theory; it is universally accepted. We know that our experiences develop or fail to develop cognitive processes. We use our vision, hearing, focus and our capacity to hold information in our minds to solve problems and to learn.

Students (and their teachers) need to understand that learning experiences change the capacity of brains to receive, perceive, understand, store, retrieve and apply information. Only then can the grit and growth mindsets unite into a learning mindset.

For example, a group of students had recently completed twelve weeks of cognitive training with BrainWare SAFARI and experienced average gains of 14 percentile points on the CogAT (Cognitive Abilities Test). They were working in a group on a challenging social studies problem. The answer eluded them for some time. One student was discouraged. "I don't think we can figure this out," he said. Another student said, "Remember how we struggled in BrainWare (the cognitive training program) and then we finally got it? I think we can do this." And they did. They solved the problem.

The core idea of Growth Mindset is that when students experience their own cognitive growth, they have the confidence to take on ever more challenging tasks. They will rebound and grow from difficulties. They will continue to want to learn.

"My favorite hobby outside of school is four-wheeling. When my family and I would ride four-wheelers, you have to know the pattern of when to switch the gears to go through the obstacles. It was really hard, in the beginning, to know when to switch gears. BrainWare SAFARI totally helped with that. I taught my brother that and my parents."

—Student at Pope John Paul II Catholic School, Lecanto, FL

Some Notes on Cognitive Skills and Mental Health

We've referred several times to students suffering from anxiety, depression and other mental health conditions. The concerns about children's mental and emotional health are front and center these days. So, we want to share a few perspectives that we think will be helpful to understand these issues in a general way. It would take a whole book, or several books, to deal with this topic, so we will simply highlight the connections we think are most important.

According to the National Alliance on Mental Illness, "The COVID-19 pandemic has presented many challenges to students, educators, and parents. Children already coping with mental health conditions have been especially vulnerable to the changes. Now we are learning about the broad impacts on students as a result of schools being closed, physically distancing guidelines and isolation, and other unexpected changes to their lives."[15]

As early as June 2020, the Coronavirus pandemic was already taking its toll on the mental wellbeing of young people.

---

15 "https://namica.org/school-during-the-pandemic-mental-health-impacts-and-help-for-students-and-families/

According to a Gallop Poll at that time,[16] "Nearly three in ten parents (29 percent) say their child is 'already experiencing harm' to their emotional or mental health because of social distancing and closures. Another 14 percent indicate their children are approaching their limits, saying they could continue social distancing a few more weeks until their mental health suffers."

Returning to the classroom has not resolved the challenges children continue to face that affect their mental health. In fact, in October 2021, the American Academy of Pediatrics, the American Academy of Child and Adolescent Psychiatry, and the Children's Hospital Association declared that the pandemic-related decline in child and adolescent mental health had become a national emergency.[17]

While COVID has exacerbated the mental health problems children were already experiencing, mental health issues were already major concerns for many parents. One often underappreciated aspect of health outcomes in general and mental health, in particular, is the role of cognitive skills. And we can look at this in two parts.

First, it is important to recognize the relationship between mental illness and cognitive functioning. Cognitive impairment commonly accompanies various mental conditions, including affective disorders such as depression, bipolar disease and anxiety. Researchers found a direct correlation between cognition and mental illness in a 2015 landmark study authored by the Mental Health Coordinating Council (New South Wales) and the University of Sydney Faculty of Health Sciences (Australia). [18]

16 https://news.gallup.com/poll/312605/parents-say-covid-harming-child-mental-health.aspx

17 https://www.aap.org/en/advocacy/child-and-adolescent-healthy-mental-development/aap-aacap-cha-declaration-of-a-national-emergency-in-child-and-adolescent-mental-health/

18 Mental Health Coordinating Council (Australia). Cognitive functioning: supporting people with mental health conditions, 2015.

More recently, a group of researchers analyzed ninety-seven studies and data from more than 200,000 individuals.[19] The study included all of the mental health disorders in the *Diagnostic and Statistical Manual of Mental Disorders*. The analysis found a link between mental disorders and cognitive dysfunction across all different types of disorders. The link holds for mental conditions from simple "worry" to more disabling disorders such as severe depression. The research team at Texas State University (Abramovitch, et.al.) coined the term "C-Factor" for this. As Abramovitch explains, "We found that both diagnosable mental disorders, as well as some common symptoms such as anxiety and worry, carry a so-called 'cognitive price.' We termed this phenomenon 'The C Factor' – short for cognitive dysfunction. This can be defined either as lower performance on cognitive tests or reduction in cognitive abilities such as attention and memory. Our analysis suggests that it can be found across disorders and that it constitutes an integral part of poorer mental health."

The effect of the C-Factor appears to be present even when an individual's mental condition is not severe enough to lead to a diagnosis. For example, many people have depressive symptoms without meeting the criteria for major depressive disorder. Diminished cognitive functioning often accompanies these symptoms. One of the reasons this is so important is that while only about 20 percent of Americans will meet the criteria for major depression, almost two-thirds will experience meaningful symptoms of depression, and therefore the C-Factor, at some point in their lives.

---

19 Amital Abramovitch, Tatiana Short and Avraham Schweiger. The C Factor: Cognitive dysfunction as a transdiagnostic dimension in psychopathology. *Clin Psychol Rev* 2021 Jun;86:102007. doi: 10.1016/j.cpr.2021.102007. Epub 2021 Mar 26.

This does not mean that deficits in cognitive skills cause these diseases and disorders. But what it does suggest is that these diseases often result in or are accompanied by lowered cognitive functioning.

And second, it is vital to recognize the potential to improve cognitive functioning, whether weaker cognitive skills are developmental or related to chronic disease, short-term stress or other causes. Examples of other causes would include brain injuries, "chemo-brain," or the "cognitive fog" that seems to be one of the long-term effects of COVID-19 in some patients.

While strengthening cognitive skills may not, by itself, cure a mental illness, developing stronger skills typically reduces stress for children and adults. This is because it gives them more confidence in their ability to learn and engage in new learning situations successfully.

In an issue brief presented by the Kennedy Forum titled *Fixing Behavioral Health Care in America: Promoting Brain Health and Brain Fitness: A National Call for Action,*[20] researchers said,

> Today we know that without interventions that directly address a child's ability to learn and function in society, our current academic paradigm and process will continue to be less than effective. Neuroscience shows that brain fitness interventions can build higher-order processing skills, promote emotional resilience, and mitigate stress.

---

20 The Kennedy Forum. Promoting Brain Health and Brain Fitness: A National Call for Action, Brain Fitness Brief, 2015.

CHAPTER SIX

Step #5   Invest in a Coach

"Olivia's coach is truly an educator. She helped our family in more ways than simply enriching our child's basic knowledge. She helped shape Olivia into the person she is today by coaching her, mentoring her and, above all, educating her, and for that, we will always be thankful! Thank you for everything you have done for us! I know your job is stressful, and to teach with such finesse, and patience ⊠ during a COVID pandemic to boot ⊠ well, we certainly admire you. You are always kind and understanding to our daughter. I am grateful to have Olivia taught by such an admirable person. You've activated a hunger in our daughter for knowledge and wisdom, inspiring Olivia to plan for her future and become a better individual. Thanks for everything. You've been so much more than a teacher for us. You've been our mentor, our support and our guide."

—William G., father of Olivia (age ten)

The Role of a Coach in Cognitive Development

We've now arrived at Step #5 of the 5 Simple Steps. Like the first four steps, Step #5 is a critical component of seeing transformation in a child's learning capacity.

The last step is to Invest in a Coach. Here it is helpful to realize that cognitive training is like a training camp for sports, but it's a training camp for learning. In their learning training camp, it's perfectly okay when children make mistakes. It is expected that learning new skills will take practice, so it's a safe place to make mistakes while you're learning. And that's one very important thing that the coach provides – creating a safe place for learning, with no judgment.

Right now, we'd like you to take just a moment and think back to a coach you once had who believed in you and inspired you in what you could do, even when you weren't sure that you could do it. Just for a moment, think about how it felt when you first did the thing your coach believed you could do. That's what every child deserves to feel as part of every learning experience.

So many children have been "beat up" by constantly feeling like a failure. They feel judged and discouraged, rather than supported and hopeful about learning experiences. All of that changes with a good coach.

Here's what we can tell you about the role of a coach in the cognitive training process.

First, the right coach will have a deep understanding of cognitive skills and their role in learning so that your child's program is tailored to their individual needs.

The right coach also understands motivation, helping your child over those inevitable rough patches, helping them tackle new challenges and supporting them as they internalize what happens when their learning skills get stronger. A significant part of this is helping your child explore and adopt effective strategies.

Coaching can also help you and your child connect their developing learning skills to whatever their educational situation looks like at any given time. And we know that has been a moving target for many families over the last couple of years.

The right coach is laser-focused on your child and helps them achieve the growth and success in their cognitive training that will carry over into everything they do.

They'll help them work through challenges and celebrate and recognize the fruits of your child's hard work that will lead to being able to do things they never thought they could do before.

You may see yourself in the image of the coach. Maybe you coach your child's tennis, or Little League Baseball, T-ball, soccer, hockey, or basketball team. Some parents relish the job of coach, and parents who have the time and inclination to be trained can also be great cognitive training coaches.

Here is a list of things that the families we work with tell us their children have experienced and benefited from directly related to their child's coach. This is a list of things that you should expect as part of the cognitive training process.

- Developing a personal relationship with an adult they can trust and work with.

- Meeting your child where they are and seeing them as a whole person. With a coach, every program and every session is designed to meet the needs of the specific child.

- Ensuring that each child's experience is designed to achieve the greatest rewards and outcomes, based on the effort and energy spent.

- Helping them understand that when they don't get something correct, it's simply that they haven't mastered that level YET.

- Helping them understand that learning is hard and sometimes a little uncomfortable; very little learning takes place in our comfort zone.

- Suggesting strategies and helping them learn which ones work best for them.

- Learning techniques to help manage frustration and anxiety.

- Developing greater personal accountability.

- Increasing willingness to take on difficult challenges.

- Developing their comfort with themselves as unique learners, recognizing that no two brains are alike, that we all learn differently.

- Emphasizing their strengths, giving them the experience of using their stronger cognitive skills, and providing strategies that leverage their strengths.

- Recognizing that a series of small steps lead to big strides.

- Emphasizing that the positive feeling of success and accomplishment come from within and are intrinsic in positive learning experiences.

- Explaining and continually reinforcing that every attempt helps their brains grow and strengthens the connections in their brain that make their cognitive skills work.

- Connecting the cognitive skills they develop in their training to everyday life, including the things they enjoy, as well as academics.

- Making learning fun.

All of this is what enables an experience that is actually transformational. And when we use the term transformation, we are referring to at least two of the word's meanings. One meaning is "a marked change in appearance or character, especially one for the better." Of course, we aren't talking about a transformation in physical appearance when we talk about cognitive skills, but in the character, function and effectiveness of cognitive skills that manifest a "marked change" that is measurable and observable.

There is another definition of "transformation" as the word is used in mathematics. In math, transformation refers to "the replacement of the variables in an algebraic expression by their values." Remember that various factors predict academic outcomes. The most important factor – the variable in the equation of academic success that has the most weight (50 percent) – is cognitive skills. When we replace the variables of cognitive skills in the learning equation, a transformation takes place. The algebraic expression actually moves to a different space.

Once again, we'd like to share a client story that helps to bring home what transformation looks and feels like. It's hard to choose because there are so many amazing stories.

CASE STUDY: CHARLIE

Charlie is a great example of the kind of hardworking student who does well in school but struggles behind the scenes. His mother, Annette, described him as a kid who looked great on paper (good grades). Still, he was struggling with anxiety and perfectionism, and it was always a battle at home to get him to do schoolwork. Once he did get started, he would do well, although getting started would take him far longer than it should have, and Annette knew there had to be something more.

Annette, despite being an educator and having a master's degree in early childhood education, found it frustrating because she knew in her heart that he was very bright. Try as she would to support him and help him stay focused, it just didn't seem to translate.

The results of his cognitive assessment made clear why that was.

Charlie's Initial Cognitive Assessment Skills Ranking

Cognitive Strengths	Skills in Expected Range	Cognitive Weaknesses
Abstract Reasoning	Working Memory	Attention
	Visual Memory	Flexible Thinking
	Spatial Perception	Verbal Memory
	Verbal Reasoning	Visual-Motor Speed
	Processing Speed	

Charlie had strong abstract reasoning ability; he could reason extremely well with nonverbal information. His other reasoning skills, working memory, and visual memory were solid. What was holding Charlie back were his attention, flexible thinking, verbal memory (which was significantly weaker than his visual memory). And his processing speed was quite low in the expected range. Knowing these weaknesses, what would we expect to see?

- A child who frequently just "gets it" and can come up with solutions to complex problems, but sometimes gets off track when he is distracted or has the answer but "forgets" to write it down (or thinks he did write it down but didn't). Check.

- A child who isn't used to having difficulty coming up with a solution, gets extremely frustrated when he gets stuck and can't come up with a different approach to a problem – something that happens to all of us, however bright. Check.

- A child who takes longer to get things done than one would expect and who seldom volunteers or raises his hand to answer a question in class. Check.

As we have emphasized throughout this book, a combination of very strong skills and much weaker skills is very, very common. Charlie is not an exception; he just felt like one. When kids have differences like this in the strength of their cognitive skills, they can't predict which learning situations will be easy and which will be hard. Every learning situation is fraught with the possibility that it won't go well. It is not surprising that Charlie also suffered from anxiety.

Imagine how frustrating it is to know the answer but always be just a little slower in coming up with it. Slow processing speed can be an especially significant concern in today's world and in our culture, where we are obsessed with speed and getting more done faster and faster. When the teacher asks a question in a classroom, some hands go up within fractions of a second. Those kids have fast processing speed, and whether or not they know the answer, that hand is up. Children with a little slower processing speed may have a very insightful answer. Still, they may not get the opportunity to share that with the class. Teachers, on average, wait 1.5 seconds to call on a student to answer. If they would slow down just by another second and a half, it's amazing what a difference that would make for a lot of kids.

At the time, neither Annette nor Charlie understood why this bright child was struggling and anxious. As Annette says, "When we started, we didn't have a way to talk about his struggles. Kids don't know why they struggle or why something is hard for them. They just struggle. Conversations about schoolwork just seemed to make him more anxious."

The cognitive assessment results changed that because it took the emotion out of the equation. As Annette says, "The results of the assessment enabled us to have meaningful conversations and help Charlie to understand his weaknesses as well as his strengths. There wasn't any of that victimization of feeling ashamed or embarrassed or threatened. It was productive."

And then came comprehensive, integrated cognitive training. Charlie also had a very significant improvement in twelve weeks of training. His processing speed went from the low end of the expected range to the middle of the expected range, as did his performance on the attention test. His flexible thinking skyrocketed. None of his scores on the post-assessment fell in the weakness range.

Charlie Cognitive Assessment Skills Ranking after Cognitive Training

Cognitive Strengths	Skills in Expected Range	Cognitive Weaknesses
Abstract Reasoning	Attention	None
Spatial Perception	Working Memory	
Visual Memory	Verbal Memory	
Flexible Thinking	Verbal Reasoning	
	Processing Speed	
	Visual-Motor Speed	

Now Charlie is able to demonstrate his powerful reasoning skills in a typical classroom setting. But it didn't stop there. Shortly afterward, he was accepted into a high school with competitive entrance standards.

As Annette describes it,

"What BrainWare has done is given Charlie an edge not only academically. He's in honors classes, and he no longer takes 1,200 hours [an exaggeration, to be sure, but the hours do seem endless to many kids and parents] to do his homework anymore. Now he handles basketball and night classes, and he's even taking AP [Advanced Placement] U.S. History. What a difference from the kid who had the ability, but who shirked away from things because of something he couldn't even express. That's the greatest thing about it. It really gets me emotional.

"I'm even involved in the field; I'm an educator. But other parents, where do they go when they don't know the first thing? They only know what schools share with them. The education system has been broken for many, many years, and we're just now starting to realize how important social-emotional learning is. BrainWare merges it together and recognizes that it's symbiotic and that's the secret sauce. I would highly recommend BrainWare to everyone, to stop using labels and to just say 'I got you. I got you.' Like I told my kid, 'I got you. Everybody learns differently, and BrainWare is going to help us find the key to unlock you and then give you all the treasures in the universe.'"

 PARENT KEY 20

Once you have a cognitive profile that describes your child "to a T," a personalized learning plan makes it actionable. You know not just what their strengths and weaknesses are, but what to do about them. (Appendix 3 looks even deeper into how these factors all fit together.)

A Message from Dr. Lou Whitaker

Lou Whitaker is an experienced educator focused on the application of neuroscience in education. She has taught students at all levels from elementary through college and graduate school and served as principal of Pope John Paul II Catholic School in Lecanto, FL. She earned her doctorate in educational leadership and administration. She has trained thousands of teachers, parents and administrators in brain-compatible education. She serves on the board of the Florida Chapter of the Association for Supervision and Curriculum Development.

We have seen dramatic improvements in students' cognitive skills. Teachers frequently comment on the difference they see in students' attention spans. And students notice changes themselves. We asked a couple of high school kids what they noticed, and it was interesting. One, who was a bright child to start with, said, "The biggest thing that I've noticed is that I would always have to go back and look at all my homework again. You have to really get it organized, you know, recheck it." As I said, he's a very good student. He said, "My memory has improved so much that I don't even have to go back and double-check everything because I've noticed I had fewer and fewer mistakes. It really helped me in that respect."

We've really noticed the changes for students who come into our school and who are behind in reading and math. One of our teachers just raved about how she saw such an improvement, and this one little child came in when she was in third grade, and now she's in fifth grade. She's just blossomed!

I've said this many times when children from low-income families come into the school. It's not that they're not bright. It's just that they were poor and didn't have the opportunities that many other children have had. When they transfer into a private school such as ours, we usually see it takes two to three years for them to get caught up to where everyone else their age level is.

Once we implemented BrainWare SAFARI, we've noticed these children within the twelve weeks they've already jumped one to two years. You've already begun to close that gap. Now, seeing her in fifth grade and how she's blossomed. I think BrainWare played a big part.

In our regular education classes, they've all participated in BrainWare. A group of students in social studies was working as a team. They had to figure out these problems, and one of the kids was getting very upset. The response from the group was, "Don't you remember Tony? Relax! It's like BrainWare. When you stick with it, you'll finally break through. We'll get it." That's what the product does.

Our clients recognize how important it is for a child to overcome their learning struggles for good. And to do that, they need a coach. If you believe in your child and their potential, you should find the best coach out there – for them. You need someone who can help you and your child start to see changes within weeks, not months or years.

What makes for a great coach – not just any coach, but the best coach for your child? You need to find someone who has the curiosity to discover the best in your child. Someone caring and concerned. Someone who can give your child (and you) the confidence to go one more round when things are challenging, and to shift and adapt strategies to reach new levels. When your child has a moment of doubt, wondering whether they have what it takes, proper coaching makes all the difference. And when they finally push through to accomplish something they never thought they could do, the coach is there to help them celebrate and to acknowledge how the effort and work have paid off.

Some parents can work with their own child to get the kind of results we've shared in this book. Other parents tell us that they feel they need a trained coach – sometimes because they don't feel they have the time – and sometimes because that parent-child relationship involves too much struggle. Kids can get pretty good at knowing how to push a parent's buttons. These same kids respond differently to a trained coach.

If you are a parent who can work with your child, we know what it takes and can support you every step of the way. If not, we know what it takes and have trained coaches who have worked with students to get the results and who develop strong relationships with their students.

"I have used this program when it first launched with my homeschooled children. This program was really helpful. Just be sure to take advantage of the training and follow instructions. If you follow the steps, you really can see results."

—Rainy B., homeschooling parent

As you consider your personal situation, keep in mind that if you don't address the situation now, the next school year will probably look a lot like this one and the one before it. Nightly homework will continue to be a nightmare. You'll continue to pay for tutoring or spend your own free time to learn what your child is supposed to be learning in school so that you try to help them just keep up. Your child may become increasingly discouraged or worse.

Or you can find the right kind of comprehensive, integrated cognitive training program, with the type of coach your child needs, and be like Charlie and the other children whose stories we've shared in the book and whose parents saw remarkable changes within weeks. The choice is yours. You don't have to be great to start. You just have to start to be great.

PARENT KEY 21

You didn't earn a Ph.D. in parenting, and
you aren't a trained educator, but you
know your child better than anyone.
There is no greater gift you can give a
child than the capacity to learn and adapt
to the changing world around them, to
bounce back from setbacks, and approach
every new experience with enthusiasm,
confidence and relish. It is a gift that gives
for a lifetime.

CHAPTER SEVEN

Hope and Transformation

"The pandemic changed the landscape of learning. Azaria was at home, and I was working from home, so she did all her classes from home and then they had the state testing. She had to go to the school to do the assessment, and she did very, very well. She got onto the Honors Roll. Not only that, we saw a definite improvement. We saw a child develop. One day she said to me, 'I want to be a paleontologist. My strength is in reading; I am still learning math.' It's just really, really good for us. Using BrainWare Learning has tremendously improved relations. It has improved the way we communicate. It has improved, I would say, even the way we play and the way we sit to eat. She is happy. We are happy. Because she gets good results, she is happy, so it makes us happy also. We see her growing as a person. We see how much more confident she is, and that is a great benefit for us. The confidence it gave her became a joy for learning. It has helped with her overall development. We are seeing a growth that we really did not expect to achieve so quickly. We are pleased, and more importantly, she is pleased."

—Pamela Coa-Jacque, mother of Azaria (age seven)

Now we need to wrap up and review the 5 Simple Steps that our clients follow to help their children overcome learning struggles and become capable, confident learners. As we do, we feel the need to underscore how different this approach is from what children are being offered in most schools and other educational settings. The education system hasn't changed in this respect as it tried to adapt to the COVID-19 pandemic, although the experience may have resulted in educators and parents perceiving greater urgency in preparing students for a changing and uncertain world.

Most of what has been written about transforming education focuses on broadening the subject matter that is taught in schools and emphasizing so-called 21st-Century Skills. Models, such as the one developed by the Partnership for 21st-Century Skills (P21) and now promoted by the Battelle Institute, seek to shift perspectives beyond traditional "academic" subjects. In these models, the "three Rs" (reading, writing and arithmetic) are no longer enough. Students are expected to learn life and career skills. They are supposed to acquire learning and innovation skills, such as critical thinking, collaboration, communication and creativity. And, it is emphasized that they will need strong information media and technology skills.

Given that the education system has not even succeeded with the "three Rs," it seems a pretty tall order for schools to add so much to what they are expected to accomplish. We don't mean to say that skills like critical thinking, collaboration, communication and creativity aren't important. In fact, they are critical. But there is an essential piece missing in the model of how these skills will be acquired.

In the P21 Model, all of the existing educational content rests on four pillars:

1. Standards and Assessments

2. Curriculum and Instruction

3. Professional Development

4. Learning Environments

Partnership for 21st-Century Skills (Battelle)

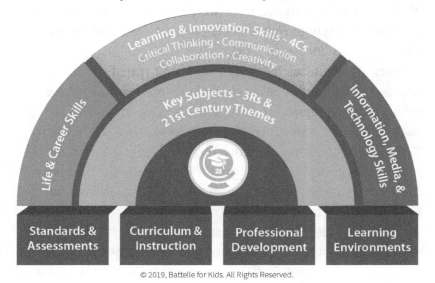

Figure 19. 21st-century skills education model.
©2019, Battelle for Kids. All Rights Reserved. www.bfk.org

What baffles us is that these are the same pillars that have always been the staples of the education system. The big question is, we believe, "Where in these pillars is the student?"

Where is the learner? The pillars are all about teaching – what gets taught, how it's taught, how it's assessed, how to improve teaching and where it gets taught (classrooms and technology). Remember the research we shared in the Introduction? All of the factors embedded in those pillars account for about 25 percent of the variance in student achievement. The factor that accounts for half – the cognitive skills that a student brings to the classroom – is not even a part of the model.

Remember …

Learning is not about pouring content into students' heads.

It is about providing them with the experiences that enable their brains to connect new knowledge into neural networks in their brains.

"The mind is not a vessel to be filled but a fire to be kindled." (Plutarch)

Most of what has been written and continues to be written about transforming education is about the external factors that impact the learning process, not the learning process itself.

Since COVID, the discussion is, unfortunately, focused more than ever on teaching rather than learning. As we pointed out in Chapter 1, the learning losses experienced by our kids are enormous. But they are dealt with as teaching losses; children just didn't experience enough teaching during the pandemic. Therefore, this way of thinking goes, we just need to figure out how to cram more teaching into their days. And somehow, in this model, they will emerge somewhere down the line knowing a bunch of stuff that the standards say they should know.

The solutions to learning loss that are being discussed – more teachers, better teachers, tutors, are again focused on everything but the learner.

Tutors and smaller group instruction do have a place. They can help fill in gaps and clarify what a student didn't understand from larger-group instruction. Tutors will typically work with a student on the next day's assignments or help the student understand material that wasn't clear to them in class. They also may help students with general study skills and organization and preparing for an upcoming test. This can give the student more confidence when they get to school for that test or for an oral presentation because the tutor has helped them organize and practice.

What tutors and other forms of extra instruction (e.g., after-school programs, summer school, helplines) generally do not do is address the underlying cognitive skills involved in learning, the most necessary ingredients in learning.

There are, fortunately, some inklings that the role of cognitive skills in subject matter acquisition is being recognized more broadly. A report from Digital Promise[21], for instance, summarizes the research on the vital contribution of these skills to learning to read.

But even as the role is being recognized, most people still think that cognitive skills are pretty much fixed – that is, you have great attention skills, or you don't. Or, if your working memory is limited, there isn't much you can do about it. However, as we've shared in this book, nothing could be further from the truth. Cognitive skills can be improved with the right kind of comprehensive, integrated cognitive training.

The goal of cognitive training is to enable a student to become a capable, independent learner. While tutoring and extra instruction can be helpful, they typically will not address underlying learning issues. Particularly when students continue to be tutored year after year, just to get through school, that is not enabling them to learn independently.

This is why the 5 Simple Steps are so important.

---

21 Shannon M Sheppard, Supporting Research-Based Personalization for Reading Success, Digital Promise, 2017. http://digitalpromise.org/wp-content/uploads/2017/07/lps-reading_success_july102017.pdf

The 5 Simple Steps: The New Way, Not the Old Way

The steps are simple, and they reflect the new way of helping children overcome learning struggles. They focus on the learner, the most important part of the learning equation. If you want different results than you've seen for your child in the past, then you have to think different, and you have to do different.

The 5 Steps are:

1. Take the Wheel

2. Set High Standards

3. Build the Cognitive Infrastructure for Learning

4. Move Beyond Grit

5. Invest in a Coach

STEP #1 – TAKE THE WHEEL

If you've gotten to this point in the book, you may very well have already taken the wheel. You embrace your job as a parent and the goal of raising a positive, proactive, self-sustaining human being who contributes to their family and society. You do it because you know that there is no one that cares more about your child than you do.

And you are now armed with a greater understanding of what learning is, why your child might be struggling with learning and the steps you can take to help them overcome those struggles, end the meltdowns, and give them the capacity and the confidence to take on challenging assignments.

The first step to making a change is taking control. If the educators in your child's world are not focused on how they learn uniquely, you need to take the wheel and drive to the future you want for your child. The old way is leaving it all to the school. The new way is to take the wheel.

STEP #2 – SET HIGH STANDARDS

We've used the words standards and expectations, and the idea of raising standards rather than relaxing them. You and your child don't have to settle for lowering the bar to make it easier to reach. Now we'd like to introduce another word that is implicit in setting high standards and expectations.

And that word is HOPE.

You know intuitively how important hope is. To be hopeless is also to be powerless. To have hope is to believe that something can change. The research on hope suggests that it has two essential elements. The first is having the will to do something. The second is having the way or ways to do it. Having the will to do something is really the first step. When you take the wheel, you embrace hope and show you have the will. The steps that follow are the ways to actually make the change and accomplish what you hope for. That's what this book has been about.

When you set high standards and expect that you and your child will find ways to help them be successful, you are far more likely to accomplish that and watch their success unfold. The old way is lowering expectations. The new way is setting high standards and providing kids with the tools to meet them. The new way also means that we can use a deep understanding of how each child learns to make the best use of the limited time and money that is available.

There is hope.

STEP# 3 – BUILD THE COGNITIVE INFRASTRUCTURE FOR LEARNING

In Chapter 4, you learned about how our brains work and develop uniquely. You learned about the cognitive skills that are the foundation for learning and how they relate to academic performance and behavior and social and emotional competence.

We then discussed how cognitive skills can be developed with the right kind of cognitive training and how that can transform learning capacity. We emphasized that every human being has the ability to learn, but that ability has to be developed into capacity.

We want to acknowledge here that there continues to be a fair amount of controversy regarding cognitive training. You will likely run across doubters and skeptics as you talk with friends and family or your child's school and others.

We actually encourage skepticism. Skepticism is generally a healthy attitude, particularly when a child's wellbeing is involved. But there's a difference between a skeptic and a doubter. A doubter rejects possibilities; the skeptic is open to possibilities and to being convinced.

COMMENTS AND QUESTIONS FROM SKEPTICS ABOUT COGNITIVE TRAINING

Here are some comments and questions we often hear from skeptics of cognitive training and the way we answer them:

I can't find enough research on the value of these programs.
Some cognitive training programs have strong research support; others have very little or no research. Look for programs supported by peer-reviewed published

research, field studies in schools or other organizations, individual/small group case studies, and a track record of results.

When it comes to research support, it should demonstrate growth both on cognitive measures as well as measures that reflect transfer to real-life application, such as academic or workplace performance.

Another question you can ask is the degree to which the research conducted is independent. Look for studies that are completely independent or mostly independent. For example, field studies in schools should have someone other than company representatives administering the assessments (often standard assessments that are already administered in those schools and not just for the purpose of evaluating the impact of the cognitive training) and conducting the cognitive training.

The peer-reviewed published research and field studies that have been conducted with our programs are available on our website at https://mybrainware.com/blog/category/research/.

How will I really know if the program is delivering meaningful results?

Many brain-training programs include built-in measures of performance and report your improvement on those measures. Unfortunately, growth on those built-in measures doesn't necessarily mean you've accomplished anything meaningful. If you work at something, like a specific brain-training game, you will most likely improve your performance on that game. But often that doesn't translate into improvements in academic or workplace performance or improved life outcomes. This is why we are such strong advocates of providing an independent, nationally normed measure of cognitive growth and using academic and other behavioral measures to evaluate the impact of cognitive training.

My child's IQ is already high. I doubt it would have much of an effect.

IQ and cognitive skills are related but not the same. An individual can perform extremely well in some areas of cognitive processing and poorly in others. For example, the term "twice exceptional" is used for individuals who have high IQs but some form of learning disability. In fact, everyone has cognitive strengths and weaknesses. Intelligence is not fixed, and cognitive skills can be strengthened, including for individuals who are already high performing. In fact, we see impacts across a wide spectrum of abilities – with more students qualifying for gifted programs and remediation of underlying skills for individuals with specific learning disabilities.

My student's IQ is low. I doubt it would have much of an effect.

This is the flip side of the question above, but the implications may be slightly different. For individuals with previous low IQ scores, it has generally been assumed that the only way for them to be successful academically is through the use of accommodations, adjustments to the curriculum and supportive strategies. These approaches all involve working around weaker cognitive skills. Of course, the idea of working around them implies that nothing much can be done to change them. But cognitive skills can be developed, as we have explained and demonstrated in this book.

The best thing about skepticism is that you leave the door open to "see it with your own eyes." One day, we got a call from a clinician working with the child of a very skeptical mother.

"I recently communicated with you about a mom who was really questioning cognitive training. Thank you for sending me the follow-up information that I shared with her. Interesting update: I just had a coaching session with the young man, and I can't tell you the positive shift I have seen in him. His mom was almost speechless with how he was performing on some of the exercises.

"The young man has dyscalculia. Now, in the exercise where you put the numbers in order, he has started doing it automatically. Before, he had strategies to visually help him, but now he doesn't need them anymore. I looked at his mom and told her, 'I'd say the program is helping him.' She nodded in agreement. She was literally open-mouthed, shaking her head at what she was seeing."

—Learning specialist

Here's to skepticism!

The old way is hit or miss. The new way is understanding your child's learning strengths and weaknesses and helping them develop their learning capacity.

STEP #4 – MOVE BEYOND GRIT

Maybe we've been a little hard on grit in this book, but we wanted to make the point that parents and teachers who tell students that all they need to do is work harder are not helping. They are adding to their children's frustration, discouragement, anxiety, and lack of self-esteem.

What we know children need instead of grit is confidence, genuine confidence in their learning skills.

THE NEW WAY

And that's what emerges from the process we characterized with this image:

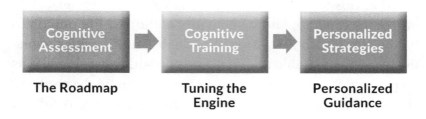

What this diagram really represents is a transformation beginning with the factors that are known to account for more of the variance in academic performance than anything else.

ACADEMIC PERFORMANCE PREDICTORS

Let's remind ourselves for a moment of some information we shared early in this book about the factors that impact academic outcomes. It is represented again here:

Predictors of Student Academic Performance

Academic Factors
25-30%

Social and Emotional Factors
20-25%

Cognitive Skills
50%

What this means is that the variables that affect academic outcomes (and we know behaviors and other life outcomes follow along with that) are the variables in this critical equation. And the variable that matters most – the one that affects 50 percent of the difference in outcomes – can be changed and changed dramatically. That's a big shift. It puts the results of the equation on a whole different plane.

STEP #5 – INVEST IN A COACH

As we've explained in this book, cognitive training is about the tools and exercises used, but it's also about the human factor. So, we've also talked about the importance of having a strong and caring coach who can help you and your child get the most out of the experience. In our work, we see that children who work with the coaches we have trained get, on average, 50 percent greater gains than those who work with their parents as coaches. However, averages are averages, and we have worked with many parents who have applied themselves to the

coach role and helped their children get results like a professional coach. Even the results "average" parent coaches help
their children achieve represent significant cognitive growth.

We'd like to share one more story that brings to life what
happens when parents follow the five steps. The transformation was Taylor's, and it started when her parents, Karla and
Vinson Higginbotham, took the wheel.

"Our daughter is introverted by nature, but I began
to notice that it was taking on a different form. It was
almost as if she was trying to disappear from the world
and society. And I knew that it didn't have anything to do
with her wanting to interact with people. I felt like she
was hiding herself so that she didn't have to perform or
say anything for fear that she would be perceived as not
knowing what she was talking about or that she wouldn't
be accepted at the same level as her friends. And that
began to concern me. I'm a teacher by trade, and I knew
that she had capabilities and that she knew the skills that
everyone else knew, but she just began to retreat.

"We had been concerned about it for about two or two
and a half years, and we have tried other things. You
know, I looked online for books that are going to help me
with this or books that are going to help me with that.
To be honest, I actually stumbled upon BrainWare by
accident. But I was very interested in it because, as I was
reading up on it, I thought this was something that could
possibly help our daughter. I thought, well, we'll just try
this and see what happens."

Taylor's mother also set high standards. She knew that Taylor had more inside her than she was able to show. She sought a program that could help uncover Taylor's special talents and enable her to become everything she felt she could be.

The process, of course, started with a cognitive assessment. Taylor's parents' ratings on the cognitive rating scale noted concerns related to accurately repeating someone's name when introduced to them, handling complex tasks without getting frustrated, not reacting impulsively, using imagination and creativity, and problem-solving. The formal cognitive assessment showed that Taylor had a good ability to sustain her attention and stronger visual memory as compared to verbal memory. Areas where she would need support included working memory, flexible attention, verbal reasoning and processing speed.

> "We were thrilled when BrainWare did the cognitive assessment on her. It told us where her weaknesses were, which were things that we had noticed at home. And we had noticed them at school. She attends a small school in a very rural area, so I'm very involved in that, and we were noticing those things. It gave us as parents something to latch onto, something to tell us this is what we need to work on. The meeting that took place was very informative, and by that, I mean they took the time to explain this is how this would look, for example, if she's not processing quickly enough or she's not hearing something. This is how that would look in the classroom if she's not processing it visually. These are the behaviors that you might see in the classroom. And so, it helped us as parents to know exactly what was going on, and that we weren't imagining things, that what we were seeing was real."

Taylor then embarked on her cognitive training with BrainWare SAFARI with her coach, Lou Whitaker. As usual, the program surfaced some areas of challenge right off the bat. Some of the exercises in BrainWare SAFARI involve clicking to a metronome beat. Timing and rhythm are challenging for many people (adults as well as kids), especially those who may have issues with attention or impulsivity. And like, many clients, Taylor couldn't "get the clicking" for a while.

> "Her initial experience with BrainWare was frustrating. One of the tasks she had to do, and we've talked about this many times, my husband and I, along with Taylor, was she had to match a rhythm. She had to click along with the rhythm, and she was struggling with that. The rhythm would come up, and it would ask her to participate, and she would attempt to do it. But then we'd hear the sound go off that she missed it. But she didn't give up. She continued to do it.
>
> "And that was amazing as a parent. And in about the second or third session, she had that rhythm, and I saw it here at the house, just the biggest smile you've ever seen, probably bigger than the state of Texas when she realized that she conquered that. And from then on, the sky was the limit. I tried to explain it to my husband when he got home that night what happened. It's hard for me to even say it without tearing up – that moment that your child knows 'I've got this.' It was just amazing. My heart was just exploding. I felt so proud. I thought, 'This is my daughter, and I knew she had it.' I knew it was inside there, and I didn't know how to work to get it where she could verbalize it and do it herself. And that's where BrainWare came in."

Developing underlying cognitive skills is what enables other skills to emerge and shine. And for Taylor, clicking to a metronome beat and working across all of the other exercises in BrainWare SAFARI was just the start.

> "We began to notice progress in her really moving through the BrainWare program about midway as she began to anticipate what was going to be required of her. We began to notice that as she was working through the program, she was becoming quicker. She was becoming more challenged, but she never gave up. That was the thing about the program. It was as if it was almost formatted for her, as if it were made especially for her. It allowed her to be her and move at her own pace and challenge herself at her own level.

> "I remember there was one activity that she did. I think she tried it 150 times before she could do it. Each time she did it, I could see from my perspective where she was in the house. I could see her determination, and I could see her sit up a little straighter and smile a little bigger when she got it. And that's when I noticed that she was beginning to build some self-esteem. The exercises were a challenge to her, and she was going to beat it, and she was going to do her dead-level best. And then it began to show in her outside activities. She belongs to several organizations, and she began to participate a little bit more. She began to open that door, and teachers began to notice, and friends began to notice. We were thrilled to death that she was even taking that step forward."

As Taylor was working in BrainWare SAFARI to strengthen under cognitive skills, she and her parents were also able to start applying personalized learning strategies keyed to her cognitive strengths and weaknesses. Taylor and her parents learned how to help her use her stronger visual memory and visual reasoning skills in her schoolwork and other activities.

> "BrainWare didn't only work with Taylor. They worked with us as parents to help us use different tactics and ways of educating her so that we could see that she could compete along with her peers."

Taylor's ability to verbalize and explain her thinking started to blossom as her cognitive skills got stronger. Her coach worked with her to develop her ability to explain her thinking as she started to solve more and more complex reasoning tasks. It started to translate to everyday conversation around the house.

> "It made me feel great. She's always been a very quiet child, and she hasn't always expressed herself. She started expressing herself around the house. She was able to talk and carry on a conversation and feel more comfortable with that."
>
> —Taylor's father, Vincent Higginbotham

When Taylor completed her cognitive training sessions, she and her parents again completed the cognitive assessments. Her scores for Working Memory, Visual Memory and Visual Motor Speed improved significantly. And her reasoning skills scores increased, especially Verbal Reasoning, which improved from an exceptional weakness to the expected range. Both parents noted significant improvement in multiple areas of processing skills, especially her confidence in her learning ability, her enjoyment of taking on challenging tasks and her ability to bounce back from failures and setbacks.

"And I can give you an example. Taylor had an interview that she needed to go to for an organization that she's a part of, to level up. In order to move up to the next level, she had to do several things, one of which was to attend a board of review. I can just tell you honestly that when we first started this, it wasn't even on her radar. It wasn't going to happen. She was pretty adamant it wasn't important to level up. Then it came time for this board of review, and she came to us, and she said, 'I'm going to do that board of review.' We weren't sure we heard her right. I think we just both looked at each other, thinking, 'What did she say?' And she said, 'I'm gonna do that board of review. I'm gonna do it.'

"She got her information together. She wrote out what she needed to do. One of the things that BrainWare did was they taught her a unique way to help herself in her learning that they called mind mapping. They thought it would be a great tool for Taylor, and they taught that to her, and they had practiced it. And Taylor, unbeknownst to us at the time, mind-mapped out all the things she felt she needed to know for this board of review.

"We took her to the meeting, and I expected to go in with her. That's always been what was necessary. I would have to go in there with her, maybe sit behind her or whatever, as her security blanket. This time, we got there and got out of the car. I was walking up to the door, and she turned around and looked at both of us, and she said, 'I've got this.' Then she went in by herself for the first time in a very, very long time. She did it on her own, and she took her mind map with her, and she passed. She passed that board of review, and she leveled up. Now there's no stopping her.

"What BrainWare did for Taylor is tell her you're unique and you can do this. That's what BrainWare did for her. It told her the sky is the limit. Here's how you learn, here's how you process, and when you use these tools, the sky's the limit."

Taylor, while she was pretty determined to begin with, was able to move beyond grit to genuine self-confidence.

Taylor and her parents also talk about Taylor's coach and how important she was in the transformation that Taylor experienced.

"Taylor's coach allowed her that growth space, allowed her to attempt it again and again and allowed her to really move through at her own pace. And we appreciated that. Dr. Whitaker was able to pick up on Taylor's personality and Taylor's fortitude. She didn't stop her, instead, she continued to encourage that 'I'm going to conquer this' attitude. And that was amazing as a parent."

It can be hard to put into words what exactly has happened when your child goes through this type of transformation and how different the experience is from anything else you or they have ever been through.

"It wasn't another book, it wasn't just another program for about six weeks and then 'It was nice, see you later.' That wasn't it at all. As a parent, you know when something's clicking with your child. You know when they take that turn. It's not really anything that you can verbalize. It's not really anything that you can describe. You just know it in your heart that something changed for Taylor. She's funny. She has something quirky to say all the time. We laugh in the house all the time now. She has stepped up and done things that we, my husband and I, we see those as miracles, and we don't have any way to explain it other than that happened through BrainWare."

When kids struggle with learning, it affects the whole family. When those struggles can be overcome, it affects the whole family. Less stress and less anxiety for the entire family, not just the child. More laughter, more smiles, more conversation, more harmonious relationships.

———————————

There you have it. In these pages, you have read how five simple steps have transformed the lives of thousands of families. It is a new way of thinking about and improving how a child learns – or how anyone learns, for that matter. Just as an athlete can train to get ready to play a sport, a learner can train to get their brain ready to learn. It's not magic; it is the leading edge of the science of learning.

We wish you every success in your journey as parents ready to follow the 5 Simple Steps to help your children overcome learning struggles and become capable, confident learners. We are confident that you can succeed with these steps. We are here to support you and cheer you on. If, at any time, you think we might be helpful, you can book a call at https://mybrainware.com/schedule/ or 877-BRAIN-10 (877-272-4610).

One thing is certain, God did not make any junk, and we can assure you he did not start with your child. There is genius in every child just trying to find a way out. You now have a path. The choice is yours!

Thank You

As we reach the end of the book, we find ourselves feeling grateful – not necessarily for finishing the last chapter – but for the opportunities we have had to reflect as we pulled all the pieces of our message together. The process has enabled us to think back to the experiences we've shared in these pages – and many others besides. We are deeply thankful for all the parents and educators who have honored us with the opportunity to help change their children's and students' lives. And for so generously sharing their stories with us.

It would take many more pages to thank, individually, all the people who have encouraged us, supported us, challenged us, and helped us learn over the years. When we started applying neuroscience to learning and teaching, it was pioneering work. When we started, neuroscientists and educators almost never collaborated. In the early days, saying that intelligence wasn't fixed and could change made some people angry (it may still do that).

One of the most fascinating aspects of the work that we have done and continue to do is that the evolving knowledge of brain structure and function has confirmed and supported the cognitive training techniques and principles that are embedded in our programs. Some principles, such as integrating skills, rather than trying to develop them in silos, were not widely accepted. Now the idea that intelligence is a whole-brain phenomenon is being demonstrated every day in new research.

We humbly appreciate the time our friends and colleagues have spent providing feedback on what we've written here. And we thank you for taking the time to listen, and, we hope, to learn.

■ Cognitive Skills Definitions

Many different mental processes or cognitive skills are important in learning and thinking. Here are definitions of forty-three skills that are some of the most important and that are developed in our cognitive training program.

ATTENTION SKILLS

Visual Sustained Attention | Auditory Sustained Attention – The ability to stay on task for sustained periods of time.

Visual Selective Attention | Auditory Selective Attention – The ability to screen out inputs other than the one that requires focus.

Divided Attention – The ability to attend to two activities at the same time, such as taking notes while listening to the teacher.

Flexible Attention – The ability to shift focus from one task to another quickly and efficiently when necessary.

VISUAL PROCESSING SKILLS

Visual Discrimination – The ability to recognize the details of an image and distinguish differences.

Visual Figure Ground – The ability to attend to a specific feature or form while maintaining an awareness of the relationship of the form to less relevant background information.

Visual Form Consistency – The ability to reorganize the visual information in a form that is consistent, regardless of object distance, location or orientation.

Directionality – The ability to interpret and project the concepts of "left" and "right" into space and onto other objects.

Visual Span – The ability to process a volume of visual information with a glance.

Visual Simultaneous Processing – The ability to combine and interpret the parts and the whole of a visual image and to recognize a pattern.

Visual Sequential Processing – The ability to see objects in a sequential order, as in reading.

Visualization – The ability to recall an image of what has been and to mentally manipulate or change aspects of that image in the mind.

Visual Processing Speed – The ability to scan, inspect and compare incoming visual information quickly.

AUDITORY PROCESSING SKILLS

Auditory Discrimination – The ability to recognize the details of sounds and distinguish differences.

Auditory Sequential Processing – The ability of the auditory perceptual processing system to send auditory information to the brain in the same order it was received.

Auditory Processing Speed – The ability to process incoming auditory information quickly.

SENSORY INTEGRATION SKILLS

Oculomotor Skill – The ability to use the eyes efficiently to read and gather information from the environment.

Visual-Motor Integration – The ability to use the eyes and hands together efficiently, as in writing, drawing, typing, catching a ball, etc.

Auditory-Motor Integration – The integration of auditory inputs and motor skills such as tapping to a beat.

Timing and Rhythm – The ability to process information at an adequate and consistent speed, the ability to appropriately pace oneself.

Visual-Auditory Integration – The ability to match auditory and visual stimuli and coordinate them into a meaningful product.

MEMORY SKILLS

Visual Sensory Memory | Auditory Sensory Memory –
The ability to screen out unimportant sensory information
and keep important information for further processing
(approximately 1/1000th of a second).

Visual Short-Term Memory | Auditory Short-Term Memory –
The ability to hold onto information in sensory memory for
up to thirty seconds until sent on for further processing or
discarded.

Visual-Spatial Memory – The ability to recall the location of
stimuli and to identify and reproduce a design.

Long-Term Memory – The ability to permanently store information and retrieve it when needed, Including semantic
information and episodic information (experiences).

Visual Sequential Memory | Auditory Sequential Memory –
The ability to recall a sequence of bits of information in the
same order as originally received.

Visual Simultaneous Memory – The ability to recall several
things received at the same time and preserve the
relationships among them.

EXECUTIVE FUNCTIONS

Working Memory – The ability to hold and manipulate information consciously in the mind.

Inhibitory Control – The ability to suppress a thought or idea and to refrain from doing something one otherwise would do.

Cognitive Flexibility – The ability to change our mindset when the rules of the world around us change, to shift between mental processes.

LOGIC AND REASONING

Visual Thinking (Reasoning) – The ability to logically and systematically transform mental images to test a hypothesis.

Verbal Thinking (Reasoning) – The ability to understand and logically work through concepts and problems presented in words.

Conceptual Thinking (Abstract Reasoning) – The ability to recognize a collection of features that go together to create an idea or category of ideas.

Logic – The ability to identify cause and effect, to reason and think rationally and analytically.

Decision Speed – The ability to use our thinking skills quickly and efficiently to make correct decisions.

HIGHER-ORDER EXECUTIVE FUNCTIONS

Planning – The ability to use forethought to create a practical and systematic strategy for attaining defined goals.

Problem-Solving – The ability to find solutions to complex issues and to constructively resolve challenges, mistakes, failures and conflicts.

Strategic Thinking – The ability to identify alternative solutions and select the solution most likely to help one attain defined objectives, keeping in mind relevant external factors and the likely consequences of one's choices.

■ 21 Parent Keys

1. Cognitive skills account for 50 percent of the variance in students' academic performance. That means that half of the difference between one child's academic performance and the child sitting next to them can be predicted by their cognitive skills. Not teachers, not class size, not curriculum or technology. So, if two students go to the same school for 13 years and one gets As, and the other gets Ds, half of that difference is explained by their learning capacity, more than any other factor. (Introduction)

2. Learning is what matters. Always focus on learning, not on teaching, accommodations or anything else. It doesn't matter how much teaching is going on if learning isn't happening. Too often, education focuses on "the what" (all the things we want children to know) rather than "the how" (how learning happens and how we can help students learn better). (Chapter 1)

3. Learning happens inside your child's brain. And every brain needs to be ready for learning. The skills that form the foundation of learning are called "cognitive skills." Cognitive skills are the processes our brains use to take in, understand, store, retrieve and apply information from the outside world. Cognitive skills are how we learn. (Chapter 1)

4. Cognitive skills can be developed to a greater degree than most of us realize. If you and your child are told that they have a weakness in one or more cognitive skill, it is not a life sentence. These are skills that can be strengthened and trained to work better and in a more integrated way. (Chapter 1)

5. Your child, like every other child, truly learns uniquely, with their own particular cognitive strengths and weaknesses. If you don't know what they are, no one can help them apply their strengths to master learning tasks that are challenging. And no one can provide just the right supports to facilitate learning and improved academic performance. (Chapter 2)

6. Learning is a biological process that involves a physical change in the brain. Learning is not about a teacher transmitting knowledge or pouring information into a student's brain. Learning is the process of each brain constructing its understanding of the world for itself. (Chapter 2)

7. There may be a lot of people willing to help your child, but there is no one that cares more than you do. Whether you brought your child into the world or brought them into your family, the connection you have is unlike any other, and there is no one else who can fill your shoes. (Chapter 2)

8. Just knowing that a child has ADHD or is on the autism spectrum or has a learning disability doesn't tell us what we need to know about how they learn. (Chapter 3)

9. The traditional approaches schools use for children with learning issues are accommodations (e.g., extra time), adjustments to the curriculum (e.g., fewer spelling words), and compensatory strategies (e.g., writing down a list of tasks). What these approaches do is help students work around weaker cognitive skills. They don't actually provide ways to strengthen those skills. (Chapter 3)

10. Intelligence is not one thing. There are many aspects of intelligence that we refer to as cognitive skills. (Chapter 3)

11. A label may indicate that a child learns differently but not what their cognitive strengths and weaknesses are. And the absence of a label means nothing whatsoever. (Chapter 3)

12. Cognitive Skills are the same mental processes whether we are using them for reading or math or having a conversation. (Chapter 3)

13. The basics are not the three R's – reading, writing and 'rithmetic, or the other subjects that are usually taught in school. Cognitive skills are the real basics for learning. (Chapter 4)

14. Cognitive skills can be developed in a comprehensive integrated system in order to reduce or eliminate the need for accommodations, curriculum modifications, and compensatory strategies. (Chapter 4)

15. We are not stuck with the cognitive skills we have. Cognitive skills can be developed with the right kind of cognitive training. Not all cognitive training is created equal. The training must embody the principles of neuroplasticity, automaticity, integration (cross-training), progressive challenge, frequency and intensity, feedback and engagement in order to develop an individual's cognitive skills comprehensively and in a way that they all work effectively together. This is how BrainWare SAFARI was built. (Chapter 4)

16. Cognitive skills are the root cause of many behavior issues as well as learning issues. Often parents and teachers misinterpret a child's behavior because they don't know what cognitive skills are involved. (Chapter 4)

17. Kids with uneven cognitive skills often have anxiety. Some learning experiences are easy, and others are inexplicably hard. They don't know why and can't predict whether something will be easy or will stump them. No wonder they're anxious. (Chapter 4)

18. Our brains use 20 percent of the energy consumed in our bodies, proportionately much more than any other part of the body. Difficult or complex mental tasks require a lot more energy than we realize. (Chapter 5)

19. "Yet" is one of the most powerful words we can use to help our children develop a growth mindset. If they are struggling with something, they can get help, or they can try a different strategy. Whenever you hear your child (or yourself) saying, "I can't do this," immediately add the word "yet." (Chapter 5)

20. Once you have a cognitive profile that describes your child "to a T," a personalized learning plan makes it actionable. You know not just what their strengths and weaknesses are, but what to do about them. (Chapter 6)

21. You didn't earn a Ph.D. in parenting, and you aren't a trained educator, but you know your child better than anyone. There is no greater gift you can give a child than the capacity to learn and adapt to the changing world around them, to bounce back from setbacks, and approach every new experience with enthusiasm, confidence and relish. It is a gift that gives for a lifetime. (Chapter 6)

APPENDIX 3

■ Cognitive Learning: A Deeper Dive

The term "cognitive learning" is used to characterize specific aspects or theories of learning and generally implies a view of learning that:

- Relates to conscious understanding rather than behavioral knowledge (skills). These two different types of learning are also referred to as declarative knowledge and procedural knowledge. Declarative knowledge refers to knowledge that can be stated and includes things like what you had for dinner last night, the date of the first moon landing, and the history of the Civil War. Procedural knowledge refers to skills that have been acquired through repetition and includes things like playing a piano piece, driving a car and decoding words.

- Explains the process of learning in terms of prior knowledge, where new information has to be connected with and integrated into existing knowledge. Existing knowledge is sometimes referred to as schemata or structures of understanding that model how the world around us works. From a neuroscience perspective, knowledge is encoded in the connections of neurons into neural networks, and new information is connected into existing networks in order to be learned and understood.

- Recognizes that cognitive processes (cognitive functions or skills) in the brain are how declarative knowledge or cognitive learning is acquired. Many discussions of cognitive learning theory address attention, sensory memory, working memory and long-term memory and the role of these cognitive skills in learning.

- Characterizes the operation of those cognitive processes on experiences the individual has and the ability of teachers (including teaching oneself) to modify the learning experience to improve the quantity, quality, depth and durability of learning.

Cognitive learning theory makes the case that we can use what we know about the cognitive processes needed for learning together with research on effective learning strategies to make learning more productive and efficient. In this context, what learners and teachers need to understand are the cognitive skills involved in learning, both generally and for that individual learner, and the types of learning experiences that are most effective in getting information through those cognitive processes, stored in long-term memory and available for use in practice.

COGNITIVE SKILLS AND LEARNING

Cognitive skills are the mental processes our brains use to take in, understand, organize, store, retrieve and use information. They include a variety of attention skills, visual processing, auditory processing, sensory integration, memory, executive functions and reasoning. Cognitive skills are the foundation of learning and account for about 50 percent of the variance in academic performance.

Cognitive Skills: The Foundation for Learning

Academic Performance Educational Attainment	Workplace Performance Lifetime Income	Health Outcomes Legal & Safety
LANGUAGE ARTS Listening, Speaking, Reading, Writing,	SEL Self-Management Social Awareness Relationships / Decisions	STEM Science, Technology Engineering, Math

Higher Order Executive Functions
Reasoning, Problem-Solving, Planning
Critical Thinking, Collaboration, Creativity
Communication

Core Executive Functions
Working Memory, Inhibitory Control,
Cognitive Flexibility

Foundational Cognitive Skills
Attention (Sustained, Selective, Flexible), Visual Processing (Visual Discrimination, Visual Span, Visual Form Consistency, Visualization), Auditory Processing, Sensory Integration (Processing Speed, Timing and Rhythm, Visual-Auditory Integration, Simultaneous and Sequential Processing), Memory (Immediate Short-Term, Short-Term, Long-Term)

For a basic understanding of cognitive skills, we recommend https://mybrainware.com/cognitive-skills/ and https://mybrainware.com/what-is-learning/.

The next thing we need to understand about cognitive skills is that every individual has cognitive strengths and weaknesses. This is what accounts for, to an under-appreciated degree, the dramatic variability in students' ability to learn different types of information.

Cognitive learning requires that teachers understand their students' cognitive profiles and that students understand their own cognitive strengths and weaknesses. It requires teachers and students to develop the ability to practice the learning strategies that are best suited to individual learning capacity.

Take the example of a student whose strengths are her reasoning skills, especially visual or abstract reasoning. For this student, the top strategy will help her use that stronger reasoning ability to understand what she is trying to learn and solve problems (apply concepts). This student has stronger visual memory (memory for images, charts, graphs) than verbal memory (memory for language-based information). Knowing this, the student will focus efforts to acquire new vocabulary on pictures and images rather than simply learning a definition. And finally, this student's executive functions, particularly working memory, processing speed and attention, are likely to be stumbling blocks. They will stand in the way of her ability to demonstrate her learning. Strategies to help her avoid distractions, organize her approach to homework, and other responsibilities will be important.

BOOSTING COGNITIVE SKILLS

In addition to adopting strategies that best fit a student's learning profile, teachers and students also need to understand that cognitive skills can be developed. Whatever cognitive strengths and weaknesses we have, we can improve our capacity to learn by strengthening our cognitive skills.

DESIGNING THE LEARNING EXPERIENCE

Since each brain must process new information for itself, the role of the instructor (whether a teacher, a trainer or an individual learning on their own) is to facilitate a learning experience that will result in efficient and effective learning for a variety of different individual brains. This is why cognitive learning focuses on the interaction of the student with the information/experience.

Interacting with material in a variety of meaningful forms will help connect it to existing neural networks (or schemata) so that is more durable and can be recalled later. Our brains did not evolve to learn meaningless information, so learning experiences need to emphasize enabling students to build meaning. This can be accomplished with activities that involve elaboration, rather than rote memorization (recall that cognitive learning focuses on declarative knowledge, not procedural knowledge where rote practice is, in fact, applicable).

Elaborative learning strategies could include activities such as:

Reciprocal or peer teaching

Metaphor and analogy

Mnemonics

Models

Storytelling

Role-playing

Problem-based learning (or project-based learning)

Developing visuals and graphics

Simulations

Hands-on activities

Rhythm, rhyme and rap

Mind maps (semantic maps)

Reflect and write (journaling)

METACOGNITION

While the term metacognition does not always appear in discussions of cognitive learning, it does capture the essence of the approach. Cognitive learning requires metacognition or thinking about one's thinking and one's progress in the learning process. It requires understanding one's cognitive skills and how to best use them in learning experiences. It requires an understanding of the learning process itself to make it deeper and more meaningful.

One definition of metacognition that captures this sense is provided by the TEAL Center (the Teaching Excellence in Adult Literacy Center, a project of the U.S. Department of Education, Office of Career, Technical, and Adult Education (OCTAE)):

> Metacognition is one's ability to use prior knowledge to plan a strategy for approaching a learning task, take necessary steps to problem solve, reflect on and evaluate results, and modify one's approach as needed. It helps learners choose the right cognitive tool for the task and plays a critical role in successful learning.[22]

This implies, like the discussion of cognitive learning above, the need to take into account individual learner variabilities, the characteristics of the learning task and the strategies one employs to facilitate the learner's experience.

---

22 TEAL Center Fact Sheet No. 4: Metacognitive Processes. https://lincs.ed.gov/sites/default/files/4_TEAL_Metacognitive.pdf

Checklist for Evaluating Cognitive Assessment and Training Programs

With the multitude of cognitive training (or brain training) options on the market today, it is helpful to keep in mind the essential components that will make a program effective and rewarding.

Evidence that it works. You should ask these three questions:

1. Where does the methodology come from? Is it speculative or has it worked?

2. Is there research that shows that the program improves cognitive skills? What skills and how much improvement has been seen?

3. Is there research that shows that the cognitive improvement translates to academic and real-life performance?

APPENDIX 4 | 221

PROGRESSIVE CHALLENGE

One of the principles of a good video game is that each level gets progressively more challenging, and that's also critical for cognitive skill development. The concept is sometimes referred to as the "Zone of Proximal Development." The user needs to be challenged but not too far above his or her current ability level. But there's more to it than simply getting more difficult at each level because what really drives cognitive growth also demands novelty and changed expectations. The program needs to include these.

COMPREHENSIVE INTEGRATED ARCHITECTURE/ CROSS-TRAINING

If a program develops skills independently, then your brain doesn't get practice at using them together. Make sure that the program you choose develops cognitive skills in a comprehensive and integrated way so that your brain will know how to "put it all together."

FEEDBACK AND COACHING

Another thing that video games do that good cognitive training programs also do is provide instantaneous feedback, which is great because we learn from our mistakes and can make immediate adjustments and try again. It's also helpful that computer feedback is not judgment. In most situations, though, a coach will drive far greater results. A coach can be a parent at home, a teacher with students at school, or someone who has been trained specifically to be a cognitive training coach. The coach needs to be highly skilled in coaching the type of user they are working with and trained in the practices and strategies of using the program to its optimum. Ask what kinds of personal coaching or training of coaches is available if that is something you want to be able to access.

ENGAGEMENT

In order for a program to deliver significant cognitive growth, it will become more challenging, likely to the point where the user will feel that they will never be able to get past the challenge. That is when engagement and the motivation to persist are essential. Cognitive training incorporating video-game elements such as themes, graphics, characters, animation, rewards and other motivational elements, supports engagement and motivation. Motivation to persist can also be fostered by good coaching and a personal relationship. The combination of extrinsic and intrinsic rewards is important for persistence and success. These determine the degree to which the program delivers on a sense of developing mastery, autonomy and an overall purpose.

PROTOCOLS TO ACHIEVE SPECIFIC GOALS

While it may look like a video game, a cognitive training program should have a regimen or protocol for usage to deliver the benefits that it claims, based on research. There may be different protocols for different goals or for different types of users, taking into consideration the frequency and intensity needed to result in changes in the strength of neural networks. Just like going to the gym once a week might make you feel less guilty, but doesn't do much for physical strength, flexibility or stamina, it will take multiple times a week for a number of weeks to make a noticeable difference with cognitive training. Make sure you know what to expect and that you will be able to follow the protocol to get the results you want. You will also want to consider how convenient the training is as a factor in how you will be able to meet the training protocol.

ASSESSMENT OF COGNITIVE GAINS

Of course, you will want to be able to measure the impact the cognitive training program has had. Some programs use progress in the activities of the program to demonstrate growth and that can be helpful. However, an objective and independent assessment, preferably one that is nationally normed (so that you can compare the individual's level of cognitive development to an appropriate peer group), is what truly demonstrates cognitive growth. So, you should ask specifically about the assessment used.

QUALITY OF CUSTOMER SUPPORT

Whatever type of program you choose, there are people behind it. Whether it's something as simple as retrieving a lost password, or something more complex like explaining the results of the assessment. Whether it's how quickly you can get started in the program, or the help you get when you feel stuck. Like any service you buy, you should feel comfortable with the support and the people involved.

■ Selected Bibliography

Abramovitch, Amital, Tatiana Short, and Avraham Schweiger. The C Factor: Cognitive dysfunction as a transdiagnostic dimension in psychopathology. *Clin Psychol Rev* 2021 Jun;86:102007. doi: 10.1016/j.cpr.2021.102007. Epub 2021 Mar 26.

Avtzon, Sarah Abitbol. Effect of Neuroscience-Based Cognitive Skill Training on Growth of Cognitive Deficits Associated with Learning Disabilities in Children Grades 2 to 4. *Learning Disabilities: A Multidisciplinary Journal,* v18 n3 p111-122 Fall 2012.

BrainFutures. Brain Fitness and Executive Function: Evidence-Based Interventions that Improve Student Outcomes. 2019.

Brookings Institution. The Impact of COVID-19 on student achievement and what it may mean for educators. 2020.

Deans for Impact. Learning by Design: Early insights from a network transforming teacher preparation. 2019.

Dorn, Emma, Bryan Hancock, Jimmy Sarakatsannis, and Ellen Viruleg, "COVID-19 and education: An emerging K-shaped recovery," McKinsey & Company, December 2021, accessed online at https://www.mckinsey.com/industries/education/our-insights/covid-19-and-education-an-emerging-k-shaped-recovery, August 3, 2022.

Duckworth, Angela. *Grit: The Power of Passion and Perseverance.* New York: Scribner, 2016.

Dweck, Carol. *MINDSET: The New Psychology of Success,* New York: Ballantine Books, 2016.

FutureEd. National, Regional Trends in Educators' Covid-Relief Spending. March 2022.

Hart, Leslie A. *Human Brain and Human Learning*. Kent, WA: Books for Educators, 1983.

Hebb, Donald O. *The Organization of Behavior: A Neuropsychological Theory*. New York: John Wiley and Sons, 1949.

Helms, Don and Sara M. Sawtelle, "A Study of the Effectiveness of Cognitive Skill Therapy in a Video-Game Format," Optometry and Vision Development, 38:1, 2007.

Holleran, L., *et al.* "The Relationship Between White Matter Microstructure and General Cognitive Ability in Patients with Schizophrenia and Healthy Participants in the ENIGMA Consortium," *American Journal of Psychiatry;* 26 Mar 2020. doi.org/10.1176/appi.ajp.2019.19030225.

Howard-Jones, Paul A. "Neuroscience and education: myths and messages." Nature Reviews Neuroscience 15, 817–824 (2014). https://doi.org/10.1038/nrn3817.

Hussar, B. and J. Zhang, S. Hein, K. Wang, A. Roberts, M. Smith, F. Bullock Mann, A. Barmer, and R. Dilig, The Condition of Education 2020, National Center for Education Statistics, 2020.

Joint Congressional Briefing on Neuroscience in the Classroom, hosted by Learning Enhancement Corporation, in cooperation with U.S. Representative Danny K. Davis, Washington, DC, January 23, 2013, Transcript of Video Recording, https://youtu.be/UoeZCQIpgX0.

Kennedy Forum. Promoting Brain Health and Brain Fitness: A National Call for ActionBrain Fitness Brief. 2015.

Macdonald, Kelly, Laura Germine, Alida Anderson, Joanna Christodoulou, and Lauren M. McGrath, "Dispelling the Myth: Training in Education or Neuroscience Decreases but Does Not Eliminate Beliefs in Neuromyths". *Frontiers in Psychology* 10 August 2017, https://doi.org/10.3389/fpsyg.2017.01314

Marzano, Robert J. A New Era of School Reform: Going Where the Research Takes Us. Mid-continent Research for Education and Learning. 2000.Mental Health Coordinating Council Inc. (Australia) Cognitive functioning: supporting people with mental health conditions. 2015.

Muller, Eve. Neuroscience and Special Education, inForum Brief Policy Analysis. National Association of State Directors of Special Education (NASDSE). 2011.

National Council for the Accreditation of Teacher Education. The Road Less Travelled. 2007.

Organisation for Economic Cooperation and Development. The High Cost of Low Educational Performance. 2010.

ParentsTogether Action. Parents Together Survey Reveals Remote Learning Is Failing Our Most Vulnerable Students. Accessed online at https://parentstogetheraction.org/2020/05/27/parentstogether-survey-reveals-remote-learning-is-failing-our-most-vulnerable-students-2/, August 3, 2022.

Rose, Todd. *The End of Average: How We Succeed in a World that Values Sameness.* New York: HarperOne, 2015.

Sheppard, Shannon M. Supporting Research-Based Personalization for Reading Success. Digital Promise. 2017.

Shenk, David. *The Genius in All of Us: New Insights into Genetics, Talent and IQ.* New York: Random House, 2011.

Siugzdaite, Roma. Joe Bathelt, Joni Holmes, Duncan E. Astle. Transdiagnostic brain mapping in developmental disorders. *Current Biology;* 27 Feb 2020. doi.org/10.1016/j.cub.2020.01.078.

TEAL Center Fact Sheet No. 4: Metacognitive Processes. https://lincs.ed.gov/sites/default/files/4_TEAL_Metacognitive.pdf

The Learning Agency. What Do Teachers Know About The Science of Learning? A Survey of Educators on How Students Learn. 2019.

Wolfe, Patricia. *Brain Matters: Translating Research into Classroom Practice,* Alexandria, VA: ASCD, 2010.

Yamamoto, Yoko and Susan D. Holloway. "Parental Expectations and Children's Academic Performance in Sociocultural Context." Educational Psychology Review 22, 189–214 (2010). https://doi.org/10.1007/s10648-010-9121-z

Zull, James. *The Art of Changing the Brain: Enriching the Practice of Teaching by Exploring the Biology of Learning.* Sterling, VA: Stylus Publishing, 2002.